15 Days of Prayer
With Saint Catherine of Siena

Also in the *15 Days of Prayer* collection:

Saint Teresa of Ávila

Pierre Teilhard de Chardin

Saint Bernard

Saint Benedict

Thomas Merton

Charles de Foucauld

Saint Francis de Sales

Saint Thérèse of Lisieux

Saint Bernadette of Lourdes

15 DAYS OF PRAYER

WITH

Saint Catherine of Siena

CHANTAL VAN DER PLANCKE
AND ANDRÉ KNOCKAERT

Translated by Victoria Hébert and Denis Sabourin

Liguori
LIGUORI, MISSOURI

Published by Liguori Publications
Liguori, Missouri
http://www.liguori.org

This book is a translation of *Prier 15 Jours Avec Catherine de Sienne*, published by Nouvelle Cité, 1996, Montrouge, France.

Library of Congress Cataloging-in-Publication Data

Plancke, Chantal van der.
    [Prier 15 jours avec Catherine de Sienne. English]
    15 days of prayer with Saint Catherine of Siena / Chantal van der Plancke and André Knockaert ; [translated by] Victoria Hébert and Denis Sabourin. — 1st English ed.
    p.   cm.
    Includes bibliographical references.
    ISBN 0-7648-0577-0 (pbk.)
    1. Catherine, of Siena, Saint, 1347–1380—Meditations. 2. Spiritual life—Catholic Church. I. Title: Fifteen days of prayer with Saint Catherine of Siena. II. Knockaert, André. III. Title.

BX4700.C4.P5313   2000
269'6—dc21   99–040108

Printed in the United States of America
04 03 02 01 00   5 4 3 2 1
First English Edition 2000

Table of Contents

How to Use This Book

AN OLD CHINESE PROVERB, or at least what I am able to recall of what is supposed to be an old Chinese proverb, goes something like this: "Even a journey of a thousand miles begins with a single step." When you think about it, the truth of the proverb is obvious. It is impossible to begin any project, let alone a journey, without taking the first step. I think it might also be true, although I cannot recall if another Chinese proverb says it, "that the first step is often the hardest." Or, as someone else once observed, "the distance between a thought and the corresponding action needed to implement the idea takes the most energy." I don't know who shared that perception with me but I am certain it was not an old Chinese master!

With this ancient proverbial wisdom, and the not-so-ancient wisdom of an unknown contemporary sage still fresh, we move from proverbs to presumptions. How do these relate to the task before us?

I am presuming that if you are reading this introduction it is because you are contemplating a journey. My presumption is that you are preparing for a spiritual journey and that you have taken at least some of the first steps necessary to prepare for this journey. I also presume, and please excuse me if I am making too many presumptions, that in your preparation for the spiritual journey you have determined that you need a guide. From deep within the recesses of your deepest self, there was something that called you to consider Catherine of Siena as a potential companion. If my presumptions are correct, may I congratulate you on this decision? I think you have made a wise choice, a choice that can be confirmed by yet another source of wisdom, the wisdom that comes from practical experience.

Even an informal poll of experienced travelers will reveal a common opinion; it is very difficult to travel alone. Some might observe that it is even foolish. Still others may be even stronger in their opinion and go so far as to insist that it is necessary to have a guide, especially when you are traveling into uncharted waters and into territory that you have not yet experienced. I am of the personal opinion that a traveling companion is welcome under all circumstances. The thought of traveling alone, to some exciting destination without someone to share the journey with does not capture my imagination or channel my enthusiasm. However, with that being noted, what is simply a matter of preference on the normal journey becomes a matter of necessity when a person embarks on a spiritual journey.

The spiritual journey, which can be the most challenging of all journeys, is experienced best with a guide, a companion, or at the very least, a friend in whom you have placed your trust. This observation is not a preference or an opinion but rather an established spiritual necessity. All of the great saints with whom I am familiar had a spiritual director or a confessor who journeyed with them. Admittedly, at times the saint might well have traveled far beyond the experience of their guide and companion but more often than not they would return to their director and reflect on their experience. Understood in this sense, the director and companion provided a valuable contribution and necessary resource.

When I was learning how to pray (a necessity for anyone who desires to be a full-time and public "religious person"), the community of men that I belong to gave me a great gift. Between my second and third year in college, I was given a one-year sabbatical, with all expenses paid and all of my personal needs met. This period of time was called novitiate. I was officially designated as a novice, a beginner in the spiritual journey, and I was assigned a "master," a person who was willing to lead me. In addition to the master, I was provided with every imaginable book and any other resource that I could possibly need. Even with all that I was provided, I did not learn how to pray because of the books and the unlimited resources, rather it was the master, the companion who was the key to the experience.

One day, after about three months of reading, of quiet and solitude, and of practicing all of the methods and descriptions of prayer that were available to me, the master called. "Put away the books, forget the method, and just listen." We went into a room, became quiet, and tried to recall the presence of God, and then, the master simply prayed out loud and permitted me to listen to his prayer. As he prayed, he revealed his hopes, his dreams, his struggles, his successes, and most of all, his relationship with God. I discovered as I listened that his prayer was deeply intimate but most of all it was self-revealing. As I learned about him, I was led through his life experience to the place where God dwells. At that moment I was able to understand a little bit about what I was supposed to do if I really wanted to pray.

The dynamic of what happened when the master called,

invited me to listen, and then revealed his innermost self to me as he communicated with God in prayer, was important. It wasn't so much that the master was trying to reveal to me what needed to be said; he was not inviting me to pray with the same words that he used, but rather that he was trying to bring me to that place within myself where prayer becomes possible. That place, a place of intimacy and of self-awareness, was a necessary stop on the journey and it was a place that I needed to be led to. I could not have easily discovered it on my own.

The purpose of the volume that you hold in your hand is to lead you, over a period of fifteen days or, maybe more realistically, fifteen prayer periods, to a place where prayer is possible. If you already have a regular experience and practice of prayer, perhaps this volume can help lead you to a deeper place, a more intimate relationship with the Lord.

It is important to note that the purpose of this book is not to lead you to a better relationship with Catherine of Siena, your spiritual companion. Although your companion will invite you to share some of their deepest and most intimate thoughts, your companion is doing so only to bring you to that place where God dwells. After all, the true measurement of a companion for the journey is that they bring you to the place where you need to be, and then they step back, out of the picture. A guide who brings you to the desired destination and then sticks around is a very unwelcome guest!

Many times I have found myself attracted to a particular idea or method for accomplishing a task, only to discover that what seemed to be inviting and helpful possessed too many details. All of my energy went to the mastery of the details and I soon lost my enthusiasm. In each instance, the book that seemed so promising ended up on my bookshelf, gathering dust. I can assure you, it is not our intention that this book end up in your bookcase, filled with promise, but unable to deliver.

There are three simple rules that need to be followed in order to use this book with a measure of satisfaction.

Place: It is important that you choose a place for reading that provides the necessary atmosphere for reflection and that does not allow for too many distractions. Whatever place you choose needs to be comfortable, have the necessary lighting, and, finally, have a sense of "welcoming" about it. You need to be able to look forward to the experience of the journey. Don't travel steerage if you know you will be more comfortable in first class and if the choice is realistic for you. On the other hand, if first class is a distraction and you feel more comfortable and more yourself in steerage, then it is in steerage that you belong.

My favorite place is an overstuffed and comfortable chair in my bedroom. There is a light over my shoulder, and the chair reclines if I feel a need to recline. Once in a while, I get lucky and the sun comes through my window and bathes the entire room in light. I have other options and other places that are available to me but this is the place that I prefer.

Time: Choose a time during the day when you are most alert and when you are most receptive to reflection, meditation, and prayer. The time that you choose is an essential component. If you are a morning person, for example, you should choose a time that is in the morning. If you are more alert in the afternoon, choose an afternoon time slot; and if evening is your preference, then by all means choose the evening. Try to avoid "peak" periods in your daily routine when you know that you might be disturbed. The time that you choose needs to be your time and needs to work for you.

It is also important that you choose how much time you will spend with your companion each day. For some it will be possible to set aside enough time in order to read and reflect on all the material that is offered for a given day. For others, it might not be possible to devote one time to the suggested material for the day, so the prayer period may need to be extended for two, three, or even more sessions. It is not important how long it takes you; it is only important that it works for you and that you remain committed to that which is possible.

For myself I have found that fifteen minutes in the early morning, while I am still in my robe and pajamas and before my morning coffee, and even before I prepare myself for the day, is the best time. No one expects to see me or to interact with me because I have not yet "announced" the fact that I am awake or even on the move. However, once someone hears me in the bathroom, then my window of opportunity is gone. It is therefore important to me that I use the time that I have identified when it is available to me.

Freedom: It may seem strange to suggest that freedom is the third necessary ingredient, but I have discovered that it is most important. By freedom I understand a certain "stance toward life," a "permission to be myself and to be gentle and understanding of who I am." I am constantly amazed at how the human person so easily sets himself or herself up for disappointment and perceived failure. We so easily make judgments about ourselves and our actions and our choices, and very often those judgments are negative, and not at all helpful.

For instance, what does it really matter if I have chosen a place and a time, and I have missed both the place and the time for three days in a row? What does it matter if I have chosen, in that twilight time before I am completely awake and still a little sleepy, to roll over and to sleep for fifteen minutes more? Does it mean that I am not serious about the journey, that I really don't want to pray, that I am just fooling myself when I say that my prayer time is important to me? Perhaps, but I prefer to believe that it simply means that I am tired and I just wanted a little more sleep. It doesn't mean anything more than that. However, if I make it mean more than that, then I can become discouraged, frustrated, and put myself into a state where I might more easily give up. "What's the use? I might as well forget all about it."

The same sense of freedom applies to the reading and the praying of this text. If I do not find the introduction to each day helpful, I don't need to read it. If I find the questions for reflection at the end of the appointed day repetitive, then I should choose to close the book and go my own way. Even if I discover that the reflection offered for the day is not the one that I prefer and that the one for the next day seems more inviting, then by all means, go on to the one for the next day.

That's it! If you apply these simple rules to your journey you should receive the maximum benefit and you will soon find yourself at your destination. But be prepared to be surprised. If you have never been on a spiritual journey you should know that the "travel brochures" and the other descriptions that you might have heard are nothing compared to the real thing. There is so much more than you can imagine.

A final prayer of blessing suggests itself:

> Lord, catch me off guard today.
> Surprise me with some moment of beauty
>   or pain
> So that at least for the moment
> I may be startled into seeing that you are
>   here in all your splendor,
> Always and everywhere,
> Barely hidden,
> Beneath,
> Beyond,
> Within this life I breathe.
>
> *Frederick Buechner*

REV. THOMAS M. SANTA, CSsR
LIGUORI, MISSOURI
FEAST OF THE PRESENTATION, 1999

A Brief Chronology of the Life of Saint Catherine of Siena

A SAINT IN A DIFFICULT ERA

When saints are presented to us individually, they are subjected to a certain image we have of them and a certain folklore surrounds their lives. We become used to seeing them as isolated characters. Their destinies seem to reveal the same logic as a novel: the extraordinary is their ordinary. This discourages us. Catherine has not escaped from this image. We must put her life into its proper context so that she can continue to exercise the special effect her enlightenment has on each person who comes to know her: from home to hospital, from castle to monastery, all the way to the ecclesiastical palaces, and beyond....

1347:   Catherine Benincasa was born to Jacopo Benincasa, a wool dyer, and his wife Lapa Piagenti, in northern Italy; she was their twenty-fourth child. She was a twin.

Catherine grew up in a good Christian home; she was diligent, cheerful, and intensely religious.

1353–1364:
Catherine had her first vision of Christ at the age of six; at the age of seven, she vowed her virginity to him.

Catherine suffered great ridicule from her family for her religious devotion and decision to never marry; she cut off her hair to make herself less appealing; her father intervened and allowed her to have a special room in the family home for prayer and devotions.

1365–1369:

Catherine was being guided in her spiritual life by the Dominicans and wished to become a tertiary, which she did, after great difficulty; she joined the Mantellate, women who were affiliated with the Dominicans and wore their habit but lived in their own homes, serving the needs of the sick and the poor under the direction of a prioress.

Catherine spent the next three years of her life in her room in seclusion from the world, devoting herself to prayer, fasting, and severe austerities in preparation for her approaching apostolate.

In 1368, Catherine ended her seclusion, convinced that Christ had accepted her as his "bride" through a "mystical wedding"; she received his command that she should bring her love for him to the world and live the gift of charity to its fullest; she worked as a nurse in homes and hospitals, caring for the ill and the poor and burying the dead.

1369–1374:

This period was spent in Siena and was marked by many important developments.

Catherine was surrounded by a vast group of friends and disciples, religious and lay alike, who called themselves her "family"; they called her "mother" as she was regarded as their spiritual leader;

It is assumed that Catherine could probably read, but it is not certain if she could write; she began her "Letters" which were all dictated to secretaries of her "family." These "Letters" started out simply as a means for spiritual education and encouragement, but soon, they began to touch on public affairs. They encouraged both the lay and religious communities. (Today, there are 382 of her letters which remain.) She spoke frankly and publicly, aroused opposition and was subjected to slander; she was accused of hypocrisy and presumption as she appeared to be a young girl with no visible skills (to the society of the time) and no social standing (due to her lack of money and unmarried state—as women of the time took their social standing from their husbands).

In 1374, she was summoned to Florence to give an account of herself to the general chapter of the Dominicans and, having satisfied their rigorous scrutiny, she and her work fell under their official protection. The Blessed Raymond of Capua was appointed as director over Catherine and her followers—this became a close association and friendship.

It is believed that she dictated her *Dialogue* during this period, but it is unclear as to the exact dates. In this, she was a woman ahead of her time, as she spoke of discernment, prayer, providence, and obedience. She dictated what God taught her in a single volume—she, in turn, taught these lessons to everyone she encountered, from the lowliest of peasants, right to the pope.

1375–1379:

Catherine had a great impact and influence on public affairs; she was led into Church politics by two important events: the Crusade and the war between Florence and her Italian allies against the papacy (1376–78).

Catherine had no direct interest in secular politics yet it is believed that her influence was mainly due to her manifest holiness, to her Dominican connection, and to the impression she made on Gregory XI and his successor, Urban VI. Gregory called her his "ombudsman," whom he sent to Florence to negotiate peace.

In 1375, in a visit to Pisa (in response to her efforts for the Crusade), Catherine had an ecstacy in a church in that city and received the stigmata, though the wounds were visible only to herself during her lifetime. They became visible to all after her death.

In 1377, she returned to Siena and, for a period of two years, continued her apostolate there and in the neighboring areas.

It was during the last four years of her life that her "Prayers" came about. In them, she spoke of God, peace, the Church, and about us with God. These were collected by her disciples.

Pope Urban summoned her, after the death of Gregory, to go to Rome; this was to be the last journey Catherine would make; she spent two years in Rome, praying and pleading Urban's cause and for the unity of the Church; she offered herself as a victim for the Church and its agony.

1380:   In the last year of her life, Catherine could no longer eat or even swallow water; she wrote a few more letters, but the majority of her time was spent in prayer and the offering of herself. Up until late February, she dragged herself the mile to St. Peter's Church each morning for Mass and spent the day there in prayer until vespers.

On February 26th, she lost the use of her legs and was confined to bed; on the 29th of April, she died at the age of thirty-three as a result of a stroke she had suffered a week earlier. Some sources say that the stroke came about as a result of her extreme distress over the state of the Church at the time.

This young, bold, and devoted woman lived her life under the triple handicap of being illiterate, lay, and a woman, in a time when not one of these characteristics was valued. She exploded the stereotypes of the times, she went where no one, let alone a woman, had ever gone before. She was adamantly against self-love and saw it as the root of all bad governments—both lay and religious.

Introduction

THE STARTING POINT OF these fifteen days together in prayer is an invitation to change direction. We often say phrases like: "I am"; "I exist"; "I love"; "I don't love"; "I live"; "I work hard"...and, at times, we sigh: "I'm fed up." In short, even when life is dull, our "I" is always at the forefront. "And God, does he exist in all of this?" The first two days of our journey together lead us to a decentering and recentering of ourselves. God said: "I am" and, with love, shows us that we "are" only because of him. This revelation forces us to change our life from one of "I" to one of "You." We have been created to contemplate and be marveled because "we are made of nothing other than love."

"The angry person says, 'God doesn't exist'" (Ps 13) because he believes that this is the price of freedom. Catherine helps us to receive our lives from the Creator because our freedom has its roots in him. Let us then enter into a knowledge of ourselves in God and of God in us. Generally, the feeling that we are nothing is seen like a descent into hell, where we fall from above: what is necessary then is an experience of emptiness where we remove ourselves from ourselves. Here, the revelation of our nothingness is a source of joy because it is given through a meeting with a God who is "enamored with his creature"—we have "nothing to do" with it!

After these first steps into knowledge and recognition, we enter even more into an intimate relationship with Christ so that we let ourselves be transformed by him. The most sure way to be like him is to look at the eagerness with which he gave himself. The shortest path is to "take the bridge"—to let go of your safety nets and let yourself be carried—and to contemplate on how freely Christ offered himself on the cross to welcome us into his open side and bathe us in his love.

The cross is the central axis of these fifteen days because it is the place that leads "to God." It was there that Christ's interior knowledge was deepened, all the way to the supreme communion: "abide in my love" (Jn 15:9). The tangible sign of this intimate relationship is Christ's blood which flows across our lives through the sacraments.

It was on the cross also that Jesus endured our lack of fidelity at a time of crisis, and the hardening of many hearts at the time of the supreme gift. Throughout these fifteen days, it is a matter of "the cloud of self-love," the temptation to abandonment and of Christ's love on the cross for the sinners that we are.

The ultimate fruit of this contemplation is the offering of ourselves—"Take my life"—for the love of Christ and his Body: the Church and all the humanity that makes up its body. This offering is etched into the amazing freedom with which Mary offered herself at the time of the Annunciation: on that day, God etched himself into this total human availability and he humbly made his dwelling amongst us.

Abbreviations Used in This Book

L: Letter
D: Dialogue
O: Prayer
LM: Legenda Major

Each is followed by a reference number for each citation, that is, D, 4 indicates *Dialogue*, number 4.

May the experts forgive us, but due to the absence of modern works about Catherine of Siena, we have chosen to use the most accessible writings available to the uninitiated public. May they be seen as a pastoral choice which has been guided by the experience of a cross section of readers.

We have shortened a few of Catherine's texts so as to not weigh down this current presentation, but we have nevertheless respected her principal ideas. The cited references are available so that the readers may refer back to the entire original text. In order to simplify the task of the reader, we have separated the sections of the prayers.

Certain meditations are concluded with actual prayers written by Catherine, others conclude with an invitation to review one's life and a conversion of the heart in the lively style as seen in Catherine's letters. You will see that they apply well to the life of the modern reader.

15 Days of Prayer
With Saint Catherine of Siena

DAY ONE

Who Am I?

I can come to know myself by identifying myself as a creature in the hands of the Creator. With this sense of humility, I can free myself of the anxiety that comes from self-importance, from saying, "everything depends on *me*!" When I come to see God as the source of all creation, the source upon which everything depends, I can accept my role as a servant of God, and love God according to this identity.

"I reply that this is the way, if you would arrive at a perfect knowledge and enjoyment of me, the eternal Truth, that you would never go outside the knowledge of yourself. and, by humbling yourself in the valley of humility, you will know me and yourself, from which knowledge you will draw all that is necessary....

"In self-knowledge, then, you will humble yourself, seeing that, in yourself, you do not even exist; for your very being, as you will learn, is derived from me, since I have loved both you and others before you were in existence; and that, through the ineffable love which I had for you, wishing to re-create you to grace, I have washed you, and re-created you in the blood of my only-begotten Son" (D, 1).

Who has never questioned his or her own identity? It dwells within us and shapes our existence to such a point that when we have a poor self-image we give ourselves up, with all our vulnerabilities, to the approval of other people and submit to the power of others. We develop an attitude of dependence with respect to people (a need for recognition, protection, warmth, affection, and so on...) and with respect to activities and things. The less I know my true self, the more I will seek ways to be recognized. It is like as if my life only exists in the eyes of others.

———

W ho am I?" is the question that Catherine asked herself at the age of about eighteen. The answer to this question would be the foundation of her spiritual life. Her personal interrogation was not born from a need for introspection. One evening, when she was totally absorbed in her conversation with the Lord, she ventured into the dialogue and suddenly, fearing she had gone too far, repented: "Miserable soul, who are you then that God would deem to converse with you face to face?... Lord, who am I? And Lord, also tell me who you are."

It was under God's scrutiny, and not that of man, that Catherine questioned herself, and it was to God that she addressed her questions. The reply would be divine. Her questioning was not born from a sense of chagrin, but from a sense of wonder (her boldness) and amazement (the face-to-face conversation between God and herself). Doesn't the possibility of a dialogue with God have the hidden risk of elevating oneself all the way to his level by sharing this sacred thing which is his Word? And when God speaks to a human person, does he not run the risk of lowering himself to a human level?

Catherine was startled by a wave of humility. She did not seek to understand herself on her own in the same way as the moon does not shine on its own. She held herself in the light of God and in the heart of her filial relationship. She received the answer: "My daughter, do you know who you are and who I am?" God's Word introduced her to the world of the beatitudes: "If you have this dual knowledge, you will be happy." Just as on the Mount of the beatitudes, after the proclamations "happy are those...," we expect to see the wisdom of the world revealed each time, but what followed can take us aback: "You are the one who is not. I am the one who is."

"You are the one who is not": that is the type of statement which should normally depress the listener, or at least offend them. But for Catherine, it had the opposite effect! The discovery of her nothingness before God would give her a freedom with respect to herself and others which would be the springboard of her apostolic boldness. Through this discovery of being nothing on her own, she received humility and gratitude.

The forgetfulness of self before "the one who is" brings the joy of knowing that everything is a blessing and the boldness to live in indebted happiness.

The obsession with a sense of self consists in lying in one's baseness. It provokes troubling feelings which are a bit nihilistic. It brings along a degradation of self and faintheartedness: under the guise of weakness, I can renounce everything; also pride, all the way until I make myself become my own judge; finally ingratitude, because under the pretext of not glorifying myself, I forget to give thanks for all that I have received.

All throughout her *Dialogue*, Catherine was amazed at the fact that we keep our existence from overflowing with the love of the Holy Trinity. It is from this love that we take our identity. We are nothing on our own. This dependence, lived with gratitude, is the secret to happiness. When we cut the umbilical cord which connects us to the Creator, when our relationship with God dwindles away, things begin to go wrong within ourselves. We tell ourselves: "I am worth nothing...I am nothing!" and we become discouraged because we see nothing other than ourselves! But from the very instant we begin to accept ourselves as creatures, created by the hands of the Creator, everything changes.

This experience is the lever of Catherine's existence. At times we are so brought down by ourselves that life weighs heavily on us...we no longer render "glory" to God. We put all the emphasis on ourselves. It is like a teeter-totter on which two persons alternately balance themselves. If we put all of the weight on God's side, naturally, we will be lifted up. It is a simple child's game. Through this elevation, we also lift up all of humanity. In Hebrew, the word "glory" signifies that which has value or "weight." When we render glory to God, we introduce this lightness into our life which comes from the fact that we put all of the weight on the side of "the One who is" and who lifts us up.

Then, life becomes a *Magnificat* and the question "who

am I?" etches itself into the refrains of lovers' songs: "What would I be without you?—Without you, I would not be! What would I be without you and without knowing with what love you love me?" Look around you and see how many people have the feeling that they exist for no one. Is that not the ultimate of dereliction? How many of them have the feeling that they exist only for themselves and by themselves? The only thing that delivers us from the "self-made person's" feeling of abandonment and solitude is to know that we only exist through God and that we are someone for him!

Throughout interchanges recorded in the *Dialogue*, the Father said to Catherine: "The knowledge of your self inspires you to humility by making you discover that alone you are nothing and that the existence that you have from me who loves you and others, before you even existed...it is this inexplicable love that I have for you which, wanting to create you again in thanksgiving, makes me wash you and give you new life by the blood of my only Son, which was spread with such a great fire of love" (D, 4).

Enter into "the room of self-knowledge" and recognize God's goodness which has given everything to you: "for in him we live and move and have our being" (Acts 17:28). "What do you have that you did not receive?" (1 Cor 4:7).

Grace will be rendered to you,
eternal Father,
to have not held me, your creature,
in contempt,
to have not turned your face away
from me nor pushed away my desires.
You, the Light, have come to me,
the shadow;
You, the life, to me , who is death;
You, the Doctor,
to my serious infirmities;
You, eternal purity, to me,
full of the dirt of innumerable sins;
You, the infinite, to me, the finite;
You, the Knowledge,
to me who is foolish
(O, 10).

Enter into your room, rid yourself of self-love. Rejoice in receiving yourself totally from the One who calls you "my daughter" or "my son." You are the one that you are for God.

Oh incomprehensible love!
Who do you call "my daughter"?
I call you "Eternal Father"!
I beg you, merciful Father,
to share the fire of your charity
with all your servants;
Your Truth said:

"Seek and you will find,
ask and we will give it to you,
knock and we will answer."
I knock at the door of your truth,
I seek,
I shout in the presence of your majesty,
I ask for your merciful clemency
for the entire world
and particularly for the Holy Church
(O, 26).

REFLECTION QUESTIONS

When I encounter my own "nothingness" when I am face to face with God, do I respond with the same kind of joy as did Catherine? Do I feel more relaxed when I realize that everything does not depend on me? Am I not comforted by the fact that God's grace is the wellspring from which I am made strong, and am able to face the trials that come into my life?

What is the nature of the self-knowledge that I possess? Am I aware of my own sinfulness? Am I still able to love myself, my neighbor, and God even knowing the depths of my own weakness and dependence? When I do possess this love, is it a selfish love arising out of my own needs and desires, or is it genuine love based on charity?

DAY TWO

The Burning Bush

Catherine was a "burning bush" to those who knew her. Catherine radiated the love of God through her words and actions. Like Catherine, may God's grace enable us to recognize the nothingness of those things to which we may presently ascribe value—those lesser goods we sometimes care for more than we care for pleasing God. May our recognition of the nothingness of these lesser goods lead us to the greatest good of all, the Everything and All that is God.

"Do you know, daughter, who you are and who I am? If you know these two things you have beatitude in your grasp. You are she who is not, and I am who is. When you have such knowledge in your soul, the enemy will no longer be able to

*defeat you, and you will escape from all of his ruses; you will
no longer agree to anything that is contrary to my commandments and will acquire each grace, truth, and light without
difficulty" (LM).*

———————

C atherine brought the Lord's answer to her question "I am
the One who is" to her confessor, Raymond of Capua. At
that time Catherine was a young girl who lived in a small room
within her paternal home. She did not leave this room for three
years for she gave herself up to prayer, living a life of fasting
and austerity.

Led by the Holy Spirit, Catherine had found for herself,
not the material cell of a hermitage, but an inner cell of her
heart in which she could always stay. Raymond noted: "She
knew how to find a desert in her own home and to make a
place of solitude in the midst of the world."

She also had temptations in her desert. Sometimes the Lord
spoke to her "like a friend speaks to another friend," sometimes it was the snake who hissed, testing her faith, her gener-
osity in her renunciations and her resolution of virginity,
through passion. She asked: "Where were you Lord when my
heart was tormented by so many disturbances?" He replied: "I
was in your heart…and who, then, caused you this sadness, if
it wasn't me who hid myself in your heart?"

In this desert, where the Holy Spirit led Catherine in the midst
of her interior tribulations, she received the revelations of God's
identity, just as did Moses before the burning bush: "I am the
one who is"—meaning that the other gods did not exist. The

idols "do not see, speak, nor hear" (see also Ps 113). They are of no help. God's revelation to Catherine is accompanied by a promise of victory over temptations and an aptitude to receive God's grace, truth, and light.

From the time of this discovery which she attributed entirely to her Creator and Redeemer, her soul caught fire. God said: "In so knowing me, the soul catches fire with unspeakable love, which in turn brings continual pain. Yet this is not a pain that troubles or shrivels up the soul, but nourishes it. Indeed, because she has known my truth as well as her own sin and her neighbor's ingratitude and blindness, the soul suffers intolerably. She suffers because she loves me, she would not suffer if she did not love me" (D, 4).

In Egypt, the bush was before Moses. It burned without consuming it. Here, the bush becomes Catherine herself, a fire that never goes out. It burns and is consumed…in prayer and the offering of herself. She was barely twenty years old and she began to inflame the people around her with little sparks. The word went from village to village, in Tuscany, then to Avignon and Rome, through her presence and through letter to letter all the way to the various courts of Europe. Who amongst us today has not been touched by her blessings? She said: "My nature is fire." Espoused by Christ in faith, she became "another 'Himself' through a union of love."

"When you and my other servants will know my Truth in this way, you will be disposed to endure all the tribulations, injuries, disgraces, in word and in deed, for the glory and honor of my name, until death. You will receive and carry worries in this way" (D, 4). Catherine never ceased putting the wood of self-knowledge on the fire of her holy desire. This is the log "that nourishes the fire of divine charity...uniting the soul with its neighbor. The more one gives fuel to the fire (that is, the word of self-knowledge) so much more increases the warmth of love for Christ and one's neighbor" (L, 219).

By the age of thirty, Catherine's life was consumed. It was consumed in compassion, that is to say in communion with Christ who suffered from the ingratitude of the people who did not see all that God had given them. The first thing that God offered them was their existence; the second was their "re-creation" through the love of Christ, who gave his life for us on the cross.

Let us pray with Catherine:

Oh eternal Father...
The light of faith
feeds the fire in my soul
and makes it grow;
make it so it can only burn
with the fire of charity
if your light only reveals
your tender love for us.
You who are the light,
you nourish and stoke the fire
in the soul
like wood nourishes a material fire.
Oh light above all other light!
Oh goodness above all goodness!
Oh knowledge above all knowledge!
Oh fire that surpasses all other fires!

For only you are the one who is,
and everything else is nothing,
if not so much it is for you
(O, 17).

Let these words penetrate into your being: "You know me in you, and from this knowledge you will take what is necessary." Release yourself from everything that does not exist.

"By knowing its nothingness, the soul is led, little by little, to know the goodness of God towards it, and from this knowledge comes a profound humility which, like a refreshing water, extinguishes the fire of pride and lights the fire of burning charity....

"The soul, by seeing God's infinite love for it, can't stop itself from loving it" (L, 43).

Recenter your entire life around the one to whom you say: "Glory be to the Father, the Son, and the Holy Spirit, to God who is...."

"You are the fire which burns forever. Oh Trinity...inflame our hearts" (O, 13).

REFLECTION QUESTIONS

What do I value most in my life? Things? People? Memories? God? What peace will embrace me when I choose God over all else in my life! Might I serve as a "burning bush" to those I encounter in my daily life? Can I radiate God's love to those people who are close to me? Who are strangers to me? In what way is God guiding me to represent his love?

DAY THREE

The Home of Self-Knowledge and of Knowledge of God

FOCUS POINT

When we look inside ourselves, aided by the light of God's grace, we can see the image of God by which we came into being. In God's image we were made, and Jesus Christ shows us what it means to be truly human through the Incarnation. We strive to know ourselves better, therefore, so that we might better understand what it means to be more Christlike, since it is the image of Christ that is imprinted upon our hearts.

"Do you know what you should do? Do as when you enter your cell at night to go to sleep. When you go to your cell, the first thing you see is your bed. You first see not only what is

necessary for the cell, but your eye and affection fly to the bed where you find rest. You should do the same by going to the cell of self-knowledge where I want you to open the eye of knowledge with affectionate love. Enter the cell and go to the bed. The sweet goodness of God is the bed. Take note that your being was given to you by grace, and not out of obligation. The sweet goodness of God is the bed. Take note that your being was given to you by grace, and not out of obligation. The bed is covered with a large blanket which is completely red in the Blood of the bleeding Lamb. Rest here and never depart.... Fatten your soul in this goodness of God.... Therefore, I beg you for the Christ crucified, remain on this sweet and glorious bed of repose" (L, 73).

In this letter to a nun beset by the devil and on the brink of giving up the fight, Catherine describes the holy cell of the twin knowledge—of God and self.

This cell is where the soul lives and also where God invites himself in. It is the spiritual dimension of existence, the place where one seeks to reconcile the thirst for the absolute with the values of the world. It is a place of interiority. At times, the soul is not always itself; there are times when either inner conflicts pursue it or the world absorbs it to such a point that it is no longer its own. It is to this holy home that the soul flees, for one has many residences, but only one home.

"*Listen!*" says the Lord. "*I am standing at the door, knocking; if you hear my voice and open the door, I will come in to you and eat with you, and you with me*" (Rev 3:20). No one has ever given proof that they respect human freedom as much as God. He who has all of the keys stands and waits at the door of his servant. Catherine marvels before the mystery of human freedom: "*He knocked at the door of your will, Oh Mary...and if you hadn't wanted to open it, God would have*

*not been incarnated in you."—"Oh Mary, temple of the Holy
Trinity, vessel of humility" (O, 21).*

*"Whenever you pray, go into your room…" (Mt 6:6). What
room? Your highest room, your upper chamber!*

▬▬▬▬

Catherine's inner room, her upper chamber, her cell, is the
home of self-knowledge. She developed biblical metaphors
in order to designate this interior life. As she was not held to
the life of a religious community, she set up a room in her
paternal home. This place became the image of the conditions
in which she lived her intimate relationship with God, in the
midst of the world.

From this home she knew everything, since it was she who
cleaned, opened the door, and served family and friends just as
would an innkeeper for Christ and the apostles. By living
Martha's grace at different levels, she lived Mary's in the room
she arranged for herself in the basement, where she heard the
Lord speak to her and give her "the best part."

By acknowledging that I am loved, I no longer recognize
myself because love has transformed me! "Oh abyss of charity, it seems that you become a fool in love with your creatures, it's as if you can't live without them, even though you
are our God. What prompts you to so much mercy? Love, and
not the need you would have for us" (O, 7). "When the soul
sees and thinks that it is so loved by God, it cannot stop itself
from loving him."

The fundamental experience of self-knowledge is not one
of failure and sin where man finds himself naked and fallen,
but one of the joy of knowing he is loved. This knowledge is

energized by man's optimism and by his trust in the freedom of always being able to do good. "God, by looking within himself, is impassioned for the beauty of his creature and, as if transported by love, he created man in his own image and likeness" (L, 210). Certainly, sin has tarnished this likeness, but the image remains the same: the marvel that I am. This knowledge is a gift. Its completion is in God: "...I will know fully, even as I have been fully known" (1 Cor 13:12).

Man, deprived of this light, becomes cruel with himself: he doesn't see that God has elevated him with so much love to a condition that is well above the one he has aspired to. He becomes a captive of his requirements and instincts, aggressive towards himself and others. He submits himself to mutilations in order to conform to the mold of his relationships and mutilates others to force their conformity to himself. The root of all cruelty towards others is then a cruelty towards himself: man has a much too diminished idea of his own dignity. He neglects himself!

When Catherine entered into the most intense phase of her apostolic life, she became more and more an itinerant without ever leaving her interior room. She suffered in a paradox: so many religious benefit from a room of stone and want to leave it for the least little pretext. Not having an interior room, many of the columns of the Church have fallen.... "I am writing to you with the desire to see you dwell in your own room of knowledge and knowledge of God about you. In this room, humility and burning charity are acquired. He who knows himself also knows God and God's goodness for him—that is why he loves God. He is not worried about the persecutions of the world, but is pleased to support the faults of his neighbor. He has made his room a heaven and he would rather stay there in the midst of the worries and the devil's temptations than find peace and rest outside.... Outside of his room, he would die, like a fish out of water" (L, 123).

Oh compassionate and
merciful Father,
have pity on us, be merciful,
for we are blind,
deprived of all light,
myself above all,
I am poor and miserable,
always cruel to myself.

Since you see all our need
in your light,
make us know your eternal goodness
so that we will love it....

The light remains at the door of the soul
and when we open it,
it floods in like the sun that hits
the closed window
and enters into the open house.

It is suitable thus that the soul would
have the will to know you
and open the eye of its intelligence;
then, oh true sun,
you enter into the soul and spread
your splendors.

You dissipate the shadows and pour
brightness in;
you chase away the humidity
of self-love
so that only the fire of charity
is left there;
you render the heart free for,
in your light,
it sees how great the freedom is that
you have given us
by removing the devil's slavery from us
where humanity lives through
its own cruelty.

Those who are blinded by self-love know nothing; not themselves, not God, and if they did, they would not be so cruel to themselves, "they would become good through your goodness."

Oh how necessary your light is!
With all my heart I beg you to give it
to all reasonable creatures
(O, 18).

REFLECTION QUESTIONS

Without the light of God's grace to reveal God's image printed upon our souls we are left in a state of self-absorption, in which there is no spiritual nourishment. Am I open to God's grace? Do I welcome this grace with the intention of knowing God on a deeper level? Do I attempt to gain self-knowledge from the perspective that I am a child of God, a child who bears the image and likeness of his or her heavenly Father?

DAY FOUR

Memory, Intelligence, and Will: Filled With God or Myself?

FOCUS POINT

Memory is a powerful tool. It can be used negatively or positively. I can choose to remember only the hurtful words and actions perpetrated against me, becoming hard and angry. On the other hand, I can choose to remember God's great love for me and his forgiveness of my transgressions against his will. Armed with this intelligence wrought from memory, I can choose to forgive as God forgives, and by God's grace love as God loves.

"He [who is ruined by the hardness of his own heart] has no remedy, because he has not used the dowry which I gave him,

giving him memory so as to remember my benefits, intellect, so as to see and know the truth, affection, so that he should love me, the Eternal Truth, whom he would have known through the use of his intellect. This is the dowry which I have given you all, and which ought to render fruit to me, the Father" (D, 4).

———

C atherine wants to make us become more capable of knowing God. She explored the operations of memory, intelligence, and will, their harmony and their conflicts. Memory has an influence upon my life. What I remember and what I forget shapes my intelligence. That which seems either clear or obscure affects the way I see myself and the way I see God and others. If my intelligence is clouded, my will becomes "disordered."

Memory, intelligence, and will, these three marvelous faculties which orient my existence are magnetized towards God. They carry the markings of God's desires, like iron filings are drawn to a magnet. Remove the magnet and the memory empties itself "of memories of God and his benevolent acts," retains nothing other than the present: "I want what I see"; or bitterness: "I can't have what I see"; or resentment: "I can't forget that." One has a short memory and believes that nothing is owed to anyone; another has the memory of an elephant, remembering only the hurts and injuries. Another drinks, does drugs, or releases pent up feelings in a vain attempt to forget.

The human memory is like a vase; its value lies in what it holds. With what do we fill it? God said: "It is the hand of love that fills the memory with memories of me and all of my benevolent acts. This memory renders the intelligence full of zeal and recognition. The soul cannot live without love. It always wants to love something. It is molded with love since I created it with love" (D, 51).

Affection nourishes my memory. Like lovers do, time and time again, it goes over the memories of all that God has given in the creation and in the alliances that he has multiplied beyond humanity's falls and disorder: "I remember and my soul overflows. If my heart grieves, I remember you" (see also Ps 42). Often the memory clings to the gifts without recognizing the donor who gives and...forgives! God said to Catherine: "That is why I hold back on my consolations at times, so that the soul will seek me and not stop itself only at my acts of benevolence." My memory could be a house of business: "I pray so that I will get...if not, I even forget to give thanks." But my memory is a temple, a place of communion with the Father who created me for eternal life...with him. By remembering the suffering of the Son, I understand my ingratitude and my transgression. By remembering the gift of the Holy Spirit to the Church and its presence in my life, my memory is amazed, my intelligence is enlightened, and my will is put into action.

Memory, intelligence, and will, all together or each through the other, keep me oriented towards God or myself, in the same way as a parabolic antenna works. I am responsible for my faculties and it is my freedom which either orients or disorients them: "When one is separated from me (God), the delicacies of the world are full of thorns and venom. As well, the intelligence is abused in its way of looking at something, the will in its love...the memory in that which it retains. There is such a strong union between these three strengths that I could not be offended by one of them without being so by the others.... One offers either good or

evil to the other according to what pleases the free adjudi-
cator" (D, 51).

There are things which are desirable and perishable—goods,
honors, consolations—which cloud the faculties. There are also
undesirable and apparently imperishable things which invade
the memory: bad memories, childhood hurts or hurtful things
that happen at any age, abandonment, ruptures, war trauma,
humiliation, accidents, sin....

Each generation has its traumatic events where every
person's life is more or less upset: some of us have known the
plague, famine, concentration camps, divorce, incest.... There
is no person's life that has not been marked by injuries or break-
ups (more or less hidden), revealed or repressed. Something
positive could come out of that: forgiveness, solidarity, mutual
understanding, conversion.... History discreetly keeps the
memory of these marvels that are so little popularized by the
media. Maybe I have been hit by the importance of evil, through
what is visible and sensory. Interior emptiness is exposed to
trouble.... "You know that something empty resonates when
we hit it, but it doesn't make a sound when it is full. It is the
same with the memory, when it is filled with the light of intelligence or loving will; you can hit it with either pleasures or
tribulations and it doesn't resonate with misplaced happiness
or impatience: it is filled with me and I am everything that is
good" (D, 54).

Each of us must learn how to manage memories of trials, they could turn into filters which leave God outside.
The cloud of self-love prevents us from seeing the grace
which is always offered to us. In her prayers, Catherine
continually remembered God and his marvels which he re-
news through everything: the creation and the redemption;
the gift of the Holy Spirit and of the Church, of the sacra-

ments and of eternal life where it is good to be with God, as much as we want.

Christian memory is like a sieve: the events which do not help us unite with God pass right through; we gather the others, just like Mary "treasured all these things in her heart" (Lk 2:51). Mary's memories did not stop at the memories of the sorrows afflicted on her Son, she became attached to her Son's love for those who did not love him. This is one way to see things. If you look back, let it be to give thanks: "Do not forget all his benefits" (see also Ps 103).

When memory, intelligence, and will are connected to God, they are inhabited by the Holy Trinity, and thus we are able to live in the image of the Triune God. By looking into the heart of man, Catherine said to herself: from whom does the memory come? From the Father, because the Father is all-powerful: everything that is, exists through him. He is the past, present, and the future. I resemble him when I remember that which—in the past, present, and future, and what I anticipate in the hope of his mercy—makes me exist. "In my heart I keep your promises" (see also Ps 119).

Catherine looks at our intelligence and asks herself: who enlightens us about ourselves, others, and the Father's will? The Wisdom of the Son. It makes us discern it through the man from Nazareth, Christ "all-God-and-all-man"; it makes us perceive love beyond the horror of the cross; our own divinity beyond our misery! "I told you, me, God, I made myself become a man and man became God through the union of my divine nature with your human nature" (D, 110).

And our will? The experience of sin has reduced it greatly: who gives us the will? The Holy Spirit. It was the Holy Spirit who gave courage to the apostles and who gives us the strength and perseverance to withstand both trials and weariness.

Thus, memory connects me to the Father, intelligence to the Wisdom of Christ and will to the Holy Spirit. I am not only surrounded by the Holy Trinity since I have been created by an overflowing of love, but I carry it within myself. Catherine comments on the word: "when two or three are gathered in my name, I am with them," by applying it to the harmony that exists between memory, intelligence, and will: when they are united in their orientation towards God, they welcome the Holy Trinity.

In God, they are three and what a harmony! In myself alone, often there is chaos.... "Unify my heart, Lord" (see also Ps 86). You who remove the sins of the world, give me peace: peace between my memory, my intelligence, and my will, so that you will have "pre-eminence in everything."

Oh unspeakable love,
the entire Holy Trinity
converged for the creation of man
and in the powers of our soul,
you fashioned us after
the very Trinity.

You gave us memory
to keep and hold what our
intelligence perceives and knows
of you, infinite goodness.
And in knowing,
our intelligence shares in the wisdom
of your only-begotten Son.

You gave us our will, gentle clemency,
Holy Spirit,
which like a hand reaches up
filled with your love
to take whatever our intelligence
knows of your unutterable goodness;
and then this will arises,
the strong hand of love,
and fills our memory and affection with you.

Thanks, thanks be to you...
that you have shown us
such great love
by fashioning us with these gracious powers
in our soul:
intelligence to know you;
memory to keep you in mind,
to hold you within ourselves;
will and love to love you more
than anything else.

How ashamed they should be, then,
those who do not love you
though they see how much
you have loved them!
(O, 1).

REFLECTION QUESTIONS

The mind is a strange and powerful tool. With what do I choose to fill my memory? Do I dwell on trivial details, business affairs, gossip, disappointments, hard feelings, failures, and fears? Or do I choose to fill my mind with the truth of God's love, his great forgiveness? And do I mold my life on this understanding of God's love, seeking to love and forgive as God has revealed, as he wants us to live?

DAY FIVE

Lift Ourselves Towards Mercy and Bow Down in the Valley of Humility

FOCUS POINT

The mercy of God is beyond all understanding, beyond every definition of justice, judgment, and love. As sinful creatures, we are not deserving of the love and forgiveness that we are given. It is pure gift, given to us from the source of unconditional love. Our focus should never be on our sin to the degree that it blinds us from the mercy of the Father. We must be humble enough to recognize our unworthiness to receive God's mercy, yet open enough to welcome that mercy into our lives.

"She [the soul] should elevate her mind in my love, with the consideration of her own defects and the blood of my only-begotten son, in which she finds the extent of my charity and the remission of her sins. And this should be done, so that self-knowledge and the consideration of her own defects should make her recognize my goodness in herself and continue her exercises with true humility.... I do not wish the soul to consider her sins...without also remembering the blood and the broadness of my mercy, for fear that she will be brought to confusion. And together with confusion would come the Devil, who has caused it under the color of contrition and displeasure of sin, and so she would arrive at eternal damnation, not only on account of her confusion, but also through the despair which would come to her because she did not seize the arm of my mercy" (D, 66).

The room of self-knowledge is an upper chamber. God gives his love according to the desire for it that his people express to him. But prayer is also the privileged place where the devil sets his traps to reign in the house. That is why God has given criteria for discernment and ways to effectively fend off the intruder.

If I consider my sins without remembering God's mercy, I will be in a state of confusion. It is "the devil's tactic" to push us towards despair under the pretext of contrition. "So for your own good, to escape his deceit and to be pleasing to me, you must, with sincere humility, keep expanding your heart and your desire in the immeasurable greatness of my mercy. In fact, you know that the devil's pride can't tolerate a spiritual humility, nor can his confusion withstand the greatness of my goodness and mercy for those whose souls are truly hopeful" (D, 66). God reminded Catherine that the devil wanted to destroy her by proving that her life had only been a deception. She reacted by picking herself up. "You do what you must do, for my goodness is never refused to one who wants to receive it. You will humbly lift yourself up towards my mercy and say: 'I confess to my creator that my life has been lived in the shadows, but I will hide myself in the wounds of the crucified Christ, I will bathe in his blood, in this way, I will consume all injustices and I will rejoice through the desire for my creator.' You know that the devil will flee."

Rather than settle for my miserable self, I will lift myself up towards mercy and hide there, with a filial trust, knowing that a son or daughter always has a place in God's heart. And I will rejoice "through the desire for my Creator"!

After the trap of discouragement, there is another which is also as seductive, self-satisfaction. God continued: "He wants to etch all of the pride by saying to you: 'you are perfect and agreeable to God, cry no longer about your faults!' I then gave you enlightenment and you saw what you had to do: humble yourself. You answer the devil: '…John the Baptist…still makes great penance; I who have committed so many sins, have I seen what this God is and how miserable I am by offending him?' The devil then, not being able to withstand either the humility of your spirit or your hope in my goodness, shouted at you: 'Curse you…. If I overwhelm you with confusion, you lift yourself up in mercy; if I praise you, you bow yourself down in humility all the way to hell and even in hell, you hit me with the stick of love!'" (D, 66). It is the devil, who was driven out of my room, that delivered the key of victory through his defeat. God bestowed upon me the ability to pursue him with the stick of love and concluded: "If you only knew of yourself alone, you would fall into discouragement; if you only knew God's goodness, you would fall into presumption."

In the home of self-knowledge, God teaches me the dangers of discouragement and self-satisfaction. In the two cases, I see nothing other than myself. In the second one, God will probably send me a few therapeutic tribulations so that I will turn myself back to him. But the first case is truly pathetic. The person who is discouraged suffers more from his fall from grace than from the offense made to God: he only has compassion for himself. The pinnacle: he judges his sin to be greater that divine mercy! The paradox of pride: in his blindness he assumes the right, in the name of his weakness, to make his "final" judgment! God also said: "Judas' discouragement saddened me more and was more devastating to my Son than his treason" (D, 137). Conversely, never forget that God dwells in you and you can always hide in the side opened for you. "If you do not become children...."

Know yourself in God and God in you. Cultivate the divine part of yourself with joy: "You are made of nothing but love."

What you feel low, lift yourself up. Christ also said to you: "Concern yourself with only me, I will concern myself with you." When "your heart is low and narrow," like Zacchaeus, climb into "the tree of the cross" (L, 119).

When satisfaction gives you a good conscience, see to it that you're not stranded in the blood that was shed for you. Bow down into the valley of humility: faced with your nothingness, God "empties" himself (Phil 2:7) more humbly than us and dwells in your room and reveals you to yourself.

Oh delicious goodness…
we only know of you
what you let us know;
and you give as much
as we are disposed
in the small vase of our soul
to receive you.
Oh very tender love,
I have not loved you
for my entire life.

I commend to you the sons
you have given me.
Alas, I must awaken them,
yet I am always asleep!
Most gentle and merciful Father,
awaken them yourself,
so that the eye of their intelligence
will always be fixed on you.

I have sinned, Lord, take pity on me.
Oh God, help us,
hurry to our rescue
(O, 18).

REFLECTION QUESTIONS

Am I aware of my sinfulness and my unworthiness to receive mercy for the sins I have committed based on the human understanding of justice and judgment? Am I aware, also, that God's mercy goes beyond all human understanding and that it is freely given by Him who has created us? Am I willing to accept this mercy? Do I forgive myself so that I can accept and welcome God's forgiveness?

DAY SIX

The River of Lies and the Bridge of Truth

FOCUS POINT

There are many obstacles on the path to the kingdom of God. Many of these obstacles are untruths, lies placed in our way by the Prince of Lies. When we begin to believe these lies is the moment we lose our way on the path to heaven. It is through *humility* that we overcome the obstacles that threaten our progress. When we recognize our limited, finite nature as creatures of the Lord, we overcome the obstacle of lies and all the falsities that attempt to convince us we are different than our true nature.

"I have told you that I have made a bridge of my Word, of my only-begotten Son. I wish you, my children, to know that the road was broken by the sin and disobedience of Adam, in such a way that no one could arrive at eternal life.... The truth is that I have created man in my own image and likeness, so that he might have eternal life and might partake of me and taste my supreme and eternal goodness. But, after sin had closed heaven and bolted the doors of mercy, the soul of man produced thorns and my creatures were in rebellion against themselves.... As soon as man had sinned, a tempestuous flood arose, which ever buffets him with its waves, bringing him weariness and trouble from himself, the devil, and the world. Everyone was drowned in the flood, because no one, by his own merit, could arrive at eternal life. And so, wishing to remedy your great evils, I have given you the bridge of my Son, so that, passing across the flood, you may not be drowned" (D, 15).

B efore leaving this world to go to his Father, Jesus said: "You know the way to the place where I am going.... I am the way, and the truth, and the life" (Jn 14:4, 6). Jesus wants to connect us with his return to the Father. With him, Catherine burned for us to take the Way beyond the waves.

Our Christian existence finds itself at the intersection of many roads. There is the one where we allow ourselves to be carried along by the world's current, like a river that flows into an ocean of death. That is the way of lies. There is the one where we allow ourselves to be carried by grace, a bridge on this impetuous river which drags so much mud along with it. That is the way of Truth. This bridge allows us to pass from one bank to another, from our kingdom to the kingdom of

God, from a life that is centered on ourselves to one that is centered on Christ. The way of Truth flows into peace and life's bounty.

Catherine, who traveled a great deal, used the language of bridges and roadways to lead us to the Father by passing by Christ. She knew the Avignon bridge, which had twenty-five arches at that time (only four remain today) and the impressive output of the Rhone River. She crossed all of the bridges on the Arno River on the way to Florence and Pisa, which were regularly subject to floods. Medieval bridges were often covered. They sheltered boutiques and, at times, a chapel. Superb specimens, they came out at the gates of the city. Even today, the construction of a suspended bridge at the mouth of a river which spans between two islands forces us to have a certain feeling of admiration. Their inauguration becomes televised news events and the media announce "it's worth the detour." But these masterpieces made by humans cannot resist the effects of time, weather and the outrage of war.

Catherine expresses Christ's mediation by using the image of a divine bridge which withstands all the floods of history. It is a bridge whose stones are cemented with his blood, because the union between his divinity and our humanity will never be destroyed, and the covenant, renewed with his blood, will never be broken. It is a covered bridge, "sheltered by mercy." It is a viaduct on which there are stations for renewal; the "boutiques" are the sacraments, in particular the Eucharist. Everything is planned in advance in order to facilitate the pilgrim's way, so that he will be nourished, his thirst will be quenched, and he will be taken care of. This bridge is a pure masterpiece of grace! Does it awaken our gratitude? Does the news of the gospel, "the detour is absolutely worth it," draw our attention? "No one comes to the Father except through me" (Jn 14:6).

From one shore to the other, God, through his Son, carries us so that we can cross the river with dry feet, like the Hebrews did at the time of the Passover. But pride removes the simplicity of crossing the bridge from us. We prefer to save ourselves on our own, leaving ourselves to drown, rather than taking the path which is opened and offered by Christ. Catherine used the image of the bridge in order to express the experience of the grace that carries us, just like Thérèse of Lisieux used the more modern image of the elevator: why would we climb the stairs and get out of breath when Christ offers us his arms to lift us up to him? The reason we do this is because we lack the humility to allow ourselves to be carried.

The bridge symbolizes the way of truth because: "lies have cut off the road to heaven." Christ, through his truth, re-established the way. At the end of the bridge, he is the gate. "I am the gate. Whoever enters by me will be saved" (Jn 10:9). The waterway symbolizes the mirror to reflect all the illusions the world has and the uncontrollable currents. "Those who cross the bridge will not drown because the water will give them nothing. The water will always flow and man will always run after the things he can neither possess nor retain" (D, 27). "It was in order to cure so much evil that I gave you my Son and I made him a bridge.... Then see what the creature owes me and how much the soul acts like an idiot because it would rather drown and not use the help that I offered it" (D, 21).

The principal subject with which Catherine was perplexed was the one of the grace that was offered and scorned. It is as if Christ hadn't come to save us; as if the bridge of his incarnation and cross had no meaning or use. "See the ignorance and blindness of man who, when we build him a road, he persists in wanting to go by way of the water. The way of the bridge is so delicious for those who follow it that all bitterness becomes sweetness and all heavy loads become light…. The joy felt by the one who follows this road cannot be adequately explained in any language, no ear could hear it, no eye could see it…. Foolish is the one who scorns such goodness by going by the lower road, where he advances in the midst of a thousand fatigues, without any consolation or goodness…. I want you, along with all my other servants, to be continuously distressed by the offenses that have been done to me, continuously compassionate towards the wrongs they have done to themselves and for the ingratitude which outrages me" (D, 28).

The question of the uniqueness of the way to go to the Father is very real. In fact, it seems that today, we can go to the Father by all roads without either passing by a Bridge or a Gate. In other words, Christ's mediation is superfluous. It is not because we affirm, according to the Gospel, that Christ is the only way to the Father that all of the other roads are condemned. We believe that all people, no matter what their belief, are children of God, love him, and can reach the Father through Christ's mediation, even if "the path" has not been revealed to them. Even if they are not specifically members of the Church, they mysteriously pass by Christ. It is so because Christ died for us and the grace to go to the Father is given "by him" to everyone.

Catherine speaks to Christians: to condemn the bridge is to reject Christ and scorn his grace. Cultivated indifference is an outrage to God's love which was manifested in Christ. Ingratitude, of which Catherine accused herself when she didn't see herself in the light of faith, is a sign that man doesn't know himself. That is why Catherine put such emphasis on this liberating truth: "I am the one who is not. You are the One who is."

Oh God of love,
you, who is truth, speaks the truth,
I know nothing to say,
I who am nothing but shadows
when I didn't seek the fruit
of the cross.
I sought and tasted the shadows....
Ah, if evil self-love
didn't make these eyes blind
which the grace of baptism enlightened!
We no longer see you,
no true goodness,
and we call what is good evil,
and what is evil good;
and thus debase ourselves
into the lowest ignorance and ingratitude.
It would have been better to have not
received the light.
A false believer is lower than a nonbeliever
and his chastisement will be worse,
yet nevertheless
he could easily run back to
the remedy and be healed
if there remains the least glimmer
of faith in him
(O, 27).

REFLECTION QUESTIONS

Do I recognize Jesus Christ as the bridge that allows me to pass over the obstacle of lies? Do I rely on the grace of God to help me identify my true nature as a creature of the Creator? Do I express my gratitude to God for this grace? Do I faithfully pray for the continued grace of God in my effort to remain humble and true to my God-given nature?

DAY SEVEN

The Bridge With Three Steps

FOCUS POINT

We are brought closer to God when we identify with the suffering Christ. When we enter into his wounded side, we are purified by his blood. And we are united to divinity. It is Christ who beckons us to the cross, for just as he thirsted for water during the crucifixion, so he also thirsts for our salvation, for our companionship in heaven.

I have told you, my daughter, that the bridge reaches from heaven to earth; this is through the union which I have made with man, whom I formed from the clay of the earth. Now learn that this bridge, my only-begotten Son, has three steps, of which two were made with the wood of the most holy cross, and the third still retains the great bitterness he tasted when he

was given gall and vinegar to drink. In these three steps you
will recognize three states of the soul....

I have said to you that, being lifted on high, he [my Son]
was not lifted out of the earth, for his divine nature is united
into one thing with it. And there is no one who could go to the
bridge until it has been lifted on high, for he said, "If I am
lifted on high, I will draw all things to me."

<hr />

Along with the revelations of the bridge of three steps,
Catherine received an invitation to climb its steps. This
bridge filled the space between heaven and the earth. It comes
from above and we climb it from below. How? Christ said:
"And I, when I am lifted up from the earth, will draw all people
to myself" (Jn 12:32)—and nothing draws love better than love.

"This bridge, which is my Son, has three steps...in these three
steps you will recognize the three states of the soul."

"The first step is the feet which signify desire. In fact, in
the same way as the feet carry the body, so does desire carry
the soul. The nailed feet serve as a step so you can reach the
side, the one in which the secret of the heart is manifested to
you. In fact, when you stand yourself up on the feet of desire,
the soul begins to feel the desire of the heart by focusing the
eye of its intelligence on the open heart of my Son; that is
where it will find perfect and unspeakable love.... The soul
then will be filled with love when it sees itself loved to this
extent" (D, 26).

On the first step, the soul bares itself of its misplaced affec-
tions in order to fix its desire on Christ. On the second, it

clothes itself with the love from which it found the secret in Christ's side. There, "the heart intoxicates itself" in such a way that one no longer sees one's self "like someone who is drunk on wine" (L, 75). The total negation of one's self leads to the next step.

"The second step climbed, the soul reaches the third, the mouth, where it finds peace after the great battle it has sustained for its own sins…. The bridge then has three steps, so that by climbing the first two, you can arrive at the last. That one is so high that the water cannot reach it. In it, there are no traces of sin" (D, 26).

These three degrees correspond to the stages of spiritual life that our religious tradition calls: purification, illumination, and union with God.

Catherine wrote to Brother Nicholas: "What a vision it is, this immense love which sacrifices itself and of itself, that is to say, from its own body, makes a ladder to draw us away from the road of sorrow to give us rest! Oh dear son who doubted that the beginning point of this road wouldn't be too difficult! But from the time that man reached the feet of affection…all bitterness became sweetness" —"That is the rule that he (God) once taught to one of his servants (Catherine) when he said: 'lift yourself up, my daughter, lift yourself up even above yourself, lift yourself up onto me. It is so that you may lift yourself up that I made a ladder for you out of my body when they nailed me to the cross. Try to lift yourself up to my feet first, that is to say, to the affection and desire for me…. It is thus that you will begin to know yourself. Then, you will reach my open side from which the wound will show you the secret: everything that I have done, I have done for the love of your heart; may your soul intoxicate itself'" (L, 64).

One day when Catherine asked Christ why he allowed his

side to be opened when he was already dead, the Lord answered that it was done in order to allow us to see "the secret of the heart," because suffering only lasts so long, while his love is infinite. "I wanted you to see the secret of the heart by showing it to you open, so that you would see that I loved you more than I could have shown you with finite suffering" (D, 75). This open side, where human beings are awaited so they can be sheltered there in tenderness, is described like a bridal suite. There is, in this contemplation, a crescendo which makes us go from the exterior to the interior. Christ not only draws us to him, but also into him: this attraction is a ravishment.

This is an admirable symbolism: when God closed Adam's side again, after having taken Eve from it (like the bone of his bone, flesh of his flesh), Catherine saw Christ's side always open so that humanity could always enter there, purify itself of its offenses, satisfy itself, and unite itself to the divinity. "The fire grows in me and I am in admiration. For I see Christians and nonbelievers enter into the crucified Christ's open side. The desire and ardor of love make me go with them, and thus enter into Christ" (L, 133).

"LET HIM KISS ME WITH THE KISSES OF HIS MOUTH!" (SONG 1:2)

The peace that Christ offers on the cross remains, even in the midst of distress and outrage: "Tribulation could attack the soul and it would not feel it. If it is in the midst of the prosperity of the world, it doesn't attach itself in an irregular manner because it bared itself of its own sense of self on the first step. That is the place where it unites itself to, and becomes like, the crucified Christ" (L, 75). "There, we taste such a meal and such a blessing that, so high up, no bitterness could reach us" (L, 74).

Could this certainty be an escape from the world? Could it be a type of tranquilizer to diminish our sensitivity to blows we have received? For Catherine, to approach Christ's mouth raises three points.

—All at once Christ cried out, "I am thirsty!" This thirst for our salvation made him suffer more than anything else. It was infinite, "while the suffering of the body is finite" (L, 8).

How can we quench him? By giving him "love for love"; by serving our neighbor all the way to facing our own death if necessary.

When do we offer him bile and vinegar? "Each time that we abandon ourselves to self-love, to negligence...when we don't stand vigil or pray much, when we are not starved for the glory of God and the salvation of souls" (L, 8).

—"When Jesus had received the wine, he said, 'It is finished.' Then he bowed his head and gave up his spirit" (Jn 19:30). That was the fulfillment. The spirit of peace which resulted was communicated to man. "Admire this patience! He didn't hear the insults which overwhelmed him on the cross. What was heard were the cries of the Jews who, on the one side shouted, 'Crucify him!' and on the other shouted at him to come down from the cross, yet he contented himself to say: 'Father, forgive them.' He remained immobile even if we told him to come down, he persevered to the end and it was with an immense joy that he shouted these words: 'Consummatum est!' (It is finished—Jn 19:30). We could believe that those were words of sadness. But they really were...words of joy" (L, 101). Christ had so wanted our salvation that he exalted in the fulfillment of his mission. True peace coincides with the Lord's joy.

—"Father, into your hands...." To welcome these last words from Christ's mouth makes us live in communion with the filial abandonment to which he had always aspired. Peace makes us live in the humility of a total giving of oneself to God.

The first step is the cloak room where you strip yourself of sin and your own will so that you want nothing other than Christ.

The second is the bridal suite where you clothe yourself with "the bridal attire of divine charity"; shocked by being so loved, you allow yourself to be consumed by this fire to the point of burning from this same love.

The third is "the peaceful bed where the soul rests" (L, 74), the place where you abandon yourself totally to God, into "the peace of obedience" because you no longer belong to yourself. The peace attained by this union is not the illusionary rest of spiritual satisfaction or apostolic laziness. Communion with Christ on the cross removes the fear of losing one's life or some advantage, it hardens the heart for the mission. "No bitterness, no sadness, no deprivation can cause distress" for the one who has received this "kiss" of peace. "He possesses supreme joy...for in God, who is supreme joy, we find neither sadness, nor bitterness" (L, 107).

Such a union not only changes our being and behavior, but also the course of history; man's relationships with others and God, their relationship to things and all of creation. "Driven by its desire for love, man's heart is drawn with all the powers of the soul: memory, intelligence, and will. Thus, harmonized and gathered in my name, all of its material or spiritual actions are drawn...and united to me through the desire for love...then it lifts itself up above to follow the crucified love"—"Thus, you see that once man is drawn, everything is drawn until everything is done for him. Therefore, the bridge must be lifted upwards and there must be steps so that we can reach it more easily" (D, 26).

REFLECTION QUESTIONS

Do I look to the suffering Christ for guidance in my life when trials seem to be overwhelming? Do I respond with love and forgiveness to the insults and hatred I encounter? Do I unite my suffering with the suffering of Jesus Christ on the cross, taking the steps laid by Christ that serve to unite creature and Creator?

DAY EIGHT

The Living Book

FOCUS POINT

The life of Christ is the "living book," and the pages are there for all to read. It is the ultimate spiritual reading, a healing book for those whose souls are sick; a book of nourishment for spirits that hunger for peace and wholeness; a book of joy for those who have known only sorrow; a book of life for those who are dead to sin. It is the book of redemption, the way to salvation.

"How do I manifest myself to the soul who loves me? My virtue is manifest in the soul in proportion to its desire.... At times I form in the mind the presence of Truth, my only-begotten Son, in many ways according to the desire of the soul. Sometimes the soul seeks me in prayer, wishing to know my power,

and I satisfy the soul by causing it to taste and see my virtue. Sometimes the soul seeks me in the wisdom of my Son, and I satisfy it by placing his wisdom before the eye of its intellect. Sometimes it seeks me in the clemency of the Holy Spirit and then my goodness causes the soul to taste the fire of divine love"(D, 147).

Illiterate, Catherine was incapable of reading books, but she was so much more gifted to read all the love that Jesus had for us on his dead and risen body. She knew the only master who was able to teach was "the gentle Truth." The Father says in the *Dialogue* that his Truth is found in holy Scripture, "which seemed dark because it was not understood; not through any defect of Scriptures, but of them who heard them, and did not understand. Wherefore I sent this light to illuminate the blind and coarse understanding, uplifting the eye of the intellect to know the Truth" (D, 147).

The Truth is a proper name of a loving person who gives of himself in order to be known. That is why knowledge is then not born from the head, but in the heart, and "love comes after knowledge." Books and outside help are useful but are dependent upon their usage. We use some means and we rejoice in Christ. But at times we prefer to rejoice in the means and use Christ. The help of a spiritual counselor or of someone who "is well-spoken" is precious, but this help could lead us to an alienating attachment instead of leading us to Christ. "Nor are you to be called instructors, for you have one instructor, the Messiah" (Mt 23:10).

Catherine, who nevertheless had spiritual counselors and maintained contact with well-read monks, often said, "What I

know does not come from any man, but from Christ." How
she touches our hearts and how many fans she has! To a priest
she replied: "I received your letter. I understand what you said.
You know that I, myself, can only see or speak of those things
which come out of my own misery, my ignorance, and my
limited intellect; the remainder comes from the sovereignty,
from the eternal Truth. The credit goes to the eternal Truth,
not to me" (L, 96).

To one of her correspondents, who was worried to
read—or to have written—a book that was suspected to be
a little unorthodox, she replied: "God has given us the eye
of intelligence and, internally, the light of faith which cannot be taken away from us, neither by the devil, nor by
creatures, if we do not lose it ourselves through self-love.
He gave us the written book, the Word, the Son of God: it
was written on the wood of the cross, not in ink, but with
blood; and its letters are the gentle and sacred wounds of
Christ. And who is the ignorant and vulgar spirit who
doesn't know to read this book? No one, except those who
love themselves, not through a lack of knowledge, but
through a lack of will" (L, 307).

"I thank you, Father, Lord of heaven and earth, because
you have hidden these things from the wise and the intelligent
and revealed them to infants..." (Lk 10:21).

"The Master has climbed to the platform of the cross, and
has taught us his doctrine that he had written on his body. He
made himself become a book whose letters are so visible that
all mankind can read them perfectly, in spite of the weakness
of their intelligence and vision. May your soul then read; may
it read and so that it may read better, may it ascend with the
feet of its affection all the way to the love of the crucified Christ;
otherwise, you will not be able to read it well. Let us arrive at

the main entrance, may we find ourselves in the wound of his side where he reveals the secret of his heart to us..." (L, 255).

We do not come to the point of loving without egoism. The rigors of the Law give us a taste for the fruit for which we fight. Saint Paul, who invites us to welcome grace, said that Christ had erased the record against us that was caused by our impossibility to follow the Law by nailing this act of accusation to the cross (see also Col 2:14). Catherine was in amazement before the crucified Christ: this document, which was all tattered, she wrote, "was made of lamb skin" (L, 251).

Oh eternal Deity...here,
memory cannot capture you,
intelligence cannot understand you,
the heart cannot love you
like it wants.
Oh divine nature, who raises the dead and
only gives life,
you wanted to unite yourself to the human
nature that was hit by death
in order to give it life.
Oh eternal Word, you united yourself to this
mortal nature
so closely that it was then impossible
to separate you from it:
on the cross the mortal nature endured the
sorrow,
but the divine nature gave it life
so well that you were both blessed and
suffering at the same time.
Even the tomb did not break apart

the union of these two natures.
Oh unspeakable mercy!
It was your own Son,
your own natural Son
that was punished
for the sins of your adopted sons!
And not only his body
endured the torture of the cross,
but his soul was tortured by desire.
Oh eternal Father,
how profound and incomprehensible your
judgments are!
An angry man cannot hear them.
Yet these angry men set themselves out to
judge your works
and the lives of your servants:
they see only the outer shell,
unable to explain
either the fathomless depth
of your love,
or the abundance of charity
poured into the souls
of your servants
(O, 27).

REFLECTION QUESTIONS

When I pray, do I contemplate the suffering Christ on the cross? Do I read from those tattered pages of the "living book," seeking the guidance and grace I need in order to rest in the eternal peace of God in heaven?

DAY NINE

The Diamond:
Misery and Mercy

FOCUS POINT

By way of the human will, choosing that which is not God, the human heart can be made hard—like a diamond. Pride, jealousy, and anger are among those obstacles the heart must overcome in its journey to God. The hardened heart is not without hope, though. The mercy of God, the love of Christ, and the blood he shed for our sake—these are the means by which our hard hearts can be softened and led to charity.

He finally came like a pleasant lamb, and seeing me, he smiled. He wanted me to give him the Sign of the Cross, and when he received it I very quietly told him: "My gentle brother, go to your eternal nuptials." He stretched himself out with great tenderness and I uncovered his neck. I was bent down towards him and reminded him of the blood of the Lamb. His mouth said nothing other than "Jesus, Catherine," and in saying these words, I caught his head in my hands.

———

Catherine wrote the above account of the death of Nicholas Tuldo, a political prisoner who had been condemned to death and with whom she stayed until his execution, to Raymond of Capua, her confessor. This young nobleman from Pérouse was so revolted by the excessive severity of his sentence that he allowed no one to come close to his desperation. It was thanks to the consolation that Catherine's visits brought him and her promise to remain with him until his execution, that he died, after his confession, "in the best disposition."

The apostle of mercy saw Christ receive the blood of the condemned man: "In this blood was the fire of holy desire that grace had hidden there." He received "his desire, his soul, that he placed in the opening of his side, in the treasure of his mercy" (L, 143).

In the aftermath of Nicholas's death, Catherine steeped herself in the powerful mystery of the Son's blood to transform the world. She proclaimed that we should hide ourselves "under the wings of the mercy of God, for it is more inclined to pardon than you are to sin. Bathe yourself in the blood of Christ."

Catherine asked God for "mercy for the world." A person's heart loses its "true north" through the injustices, wars, sufferings, and indignities of the world. "Fools say in their hearts: there is no God!" (Ps 53:1). At times, the soul closes itself like an oyster: "Our plot is perfect. Each of our hearts remains impenetrable" (see also Ps 33).

Catherine did not need to read newspapers or watch televised newscasts in order to spend her days and nights praying for intercessions for sinners and those with hardened hearts. She took care of the poor and the sick and, in this world of misery, she was, above all, sensitive to the sicknesses of the soul. Envy, hatred, jealousy, oppression, and bitterness are the hidden faces of society's evils. She knew of the vanity of the princes of the Church, the lukewarmness of the religious, and the vainglory of the governors. Time was short, there were frequent assassinations. She saw the passage of cartloads of people condemned to death. But what anguished her was not so much their crimes or debaucheries, but the unrepentant powerful and the lack of hope on the faces of the lost children who she wanted to help. She reflected on the salvational love of her Redeemer, united herself to his intentions, and suffered the death and passion with him to see that the blood of Christ flowed onto the ground and that his love was scorned and that man preferred his own self-love. She wanted to do nothing other than work for the salvation of souls: she recommended that her confessor "be pleased to be with the tax-collectors and sinners; as for the others, love them a great deal, but see them little"!

There is a permanent contrast in Catherine's message between Christ's open side and man's closed heart. Those who persist in hardness, ingratitude, or despair "have imposed on their heart, with the hand of free will, a diamondlike hardness which, if it is not broken with blood, will never be broken" (D, 4). The diamond: the hardest of all stones! Nothing is more resistent. Catherine has the same message for everyone: criminals, cynics, angered people, those in despair, and those consecrated souls who have become hardened by a lack of charity: "I beg you, on behalf of the crucified Christ, may this stone dissolve itself through the abundance of the generous blood of the Son of God. His warmth is so great that there is no coldness or hardness that can resist it" (L, 146, to an abbess). Pope and archbishop alike, all must submit themselves: their hearts of stone must melt before the love of the crucified one!

Exposed to the sarcasms of his people, Christ promised the kingdom to the penitent thief. "A broken and contrite heart, O God, you will not despise" (Ps 51:17). "Today, do not close your heart, but hear the Lord's voice" (see also Ps 93). "Take care, brothers and sisters, that none of you may have an evil, unbelieving heart that turns away from the living God. But exhort one another every day, as long as it is called 'today' so that none of you may be hardened by the deceitfulness of sin" (Heb 3:12–13).

For some, their hearts are so hardened that the diamond becomes their tombstone: they are deposited in the shadow of death. Their removal from the tomb could only come through an act of God, the rising Sun which comes to visit us. It is through prayer that Catherine obtained conversions. The conversion of Nanni, a criminal nobleman, whose heart had been petrified by mortal hatreds, showed how it happened: she used "each one of the words which injured and those which put oil on the wound; but he, like a snake that couldn't hear, completely closed the ear of his heart." As soon as the Holy Spirit yielded a point, he entered through the breech. The ramparts collapsed. The man "cracked" and placed himself into the hands of the transpierced one. Catherine confided to him: "Beloved brother, the Lord's mercy finally made you recognize the danger you were in. I spoke to you and you scorned my words. I then addressed myself to the Lord, who did not scorn my prayer. Make penance...for fear that you won't be surprised by trials" (Life II, 7).

Our modern times have nothing to envy about the mortal hatreds of the Middle Ages. Civil justice and politics imposed truces. But the times forced a fermentation of sorts, under the cornerstone of "the stench of souls," to the point that the boiling pot of the people exploded anew: with revenge, genocides, ethnic purifications, torture.... In ecclesiastic and familial conflicts, time does not heal. To the contrary, it digs a pit. Only love and mercy breaks hardened hearts and swords.

Catherine obtained conversions through prayer and preaching: she demanded perfect penitence for each person. Brother Raymond reported that, during one of her peacemaking missions in Siena county, he saw hundreds of people come down from the mountains as if they had been summoned by an "invisible trumpet." When they saw Catherine, the people were as touched by her preaching as the Jews were by that of Peter about the crucified Christ: "Now when they heard this, they were cut to the heart and said: 'What should we do?' (...) 'Repent'" (Acts 2:37–38). Peter left the temple, Catherine left her interior room. Raymond continued: "I was one of her confessors, and I found such vivid penitence among the penitents that no one could doubt the great abundance of grace that descended from heaven in their hearts." This was not a unique incident since, in 1376, Pope Gregory XI had, through an apostolic bull, accorded Catherine the services of three confessors to accompany her and these confessors were in possession of special powers to absolve the greatest of sinners who were heavily laden. The majority of them had never made a confession or had never approached Christ's mercy with an open heart....

Go into your interior room and beg for mercy for the Church and the world.

Through the sacraments, you have received Christ's blood into your heart. Does not negligence make it harden like marble? To you as well, Christ said: "Open yourself and make room, I will make myself become a torrent."

"I was sick and you took care of me, I was in prison and you visited me" (Mt 25:36). Do those who are sick because of their hardness and prisoners because of their stubbornness have a place in your affection and your prayer or is it your heart that must be tender? "There is nothing colder that a Christian who is indifferent to the salvation of others" (John Chrysostom).

REFLECTION QUESTIONS

Is there a place for greater charity in my life? Do I pray to Jesus Christ that he soften the hardness of my heart? What can I do to allow his grace into my life? What petty jealousy, pride, and anger can I let go of in order to set my sights on the mercy of God? What acts of charity can I attempt that may have frightened me before?

DAY TEN

The Flies Flee the Fire

FOCUS POINT

The soul that is lax and without ardor for the love of God is susceptible to attacks from the devil. As Jesus had spoken of in Scripture, the devil finds an empty place, all swept and prepared, ready to be occupied. And since the space is not presently occupied with love for God, there is a vacancy the devil seeks to fill in our soul. But if this soul is inflamed with love for God, the devil can find no place there—it is on fire for God.

"It is indeed true that the devil never sleeps but teaches you, if you are careless, to sleep when it is profitable to him. But his watching cannot hurt these [that is, those who, united to God by full conformity of their will with the divine will, are con-

cerned neither with consolations nor tribulations]...for he can-
not stand the heat of charity, nor the fragrance of their soul's
union with me, the sea of peace. No, the soul cannot be tricked
so long as it remains united to me. So the devil flees like a fly
from a boiling pot, because he is afraid of the fire. If the soul
were lukewarm he would enter fearlessly though often he per-
ishes there when he finds it hotter than he had imagined" (D,
90).

Catherine's heart became inflamed when faced with Christ's love: "This fire which, up until now, was smoldering under our own cinders, began to manifest itself in a big way when his most blessed body was half-opened on the wood of the cross, so that the attraction of the soul would be carried towards the heights, and the glance of its intelligence could discern the fire of love" (O, 22).

At times we think that it was the evilness of man that vanquished Christ on the cross. At least that is what it seems to be to us. But for Catherine, only "the most holy charity could triumph over God," not sin. Not even the instruments of torture, because "the nails were unable to affix him to the cross. There was only one sole connection that could keep him there, charity" (L, 126).

If we meditate on the love that God has for us, no other human or devil could limit our desire "for the honor of God and the salvation of mankind." Because the devils run away from the ones whose hearts were inflamed with divine love, they flee like insects before a burning pot. But if it is lukewarm, then the flies run rampant, moving in and feeding off it.

At times, Catherine continued, the flies entered into the

pot and soon left it because it was even hotter than they could imagine. Thus, the devil enters the soul, believing it to be luke-warm. He enters it through numerous temptations, but leaves it again when he sees the soul's ardor, "in the process of know-ing itself and understanding the pain of its sins." The soul, united to God and inflamed with the holy will, makes the devil flee like flies flee from the pot on the fire because they are afraid to get burned.

The Flies, a drama in three acts, was Jean Paul Sartre's first work. It showcases freedom in action. Millions of flies had been sent to the town of Argos by the gods since Égisthe had killed the king. They are symbols of remorse which weigh heavily....

The flies, like all insect invasions, are a plague. They sym-bolize what is undesirable, the numerous assaults of the devil. In Catherine's *Dialogue*, the Father exhorts her to meet this situation with ardor. He even invites us to rejoice in finding it there, "for in battle, the soul will best know that God dwells in it. How? I am going to tell you: it knows that, at the time of battle, it cannot escape, nor can it do what will not be done. It is then that it recognizes that it is nothing. Its will could simply be to refuse to consent to it: nothing else. If it was something on its own, it would get rid of what it doesn't want. It is thus that it becomes humble through the true recognition of its self. It is with the light of most holy faith that it runs towards me, eternal God, whose goodness keeps its good will for it and prevents it from yielding to the miseries which torment it at the moment of battle" (D, 90).

At times "of tribulations, adversity, or temptations by man or the devil," only ardor chases the flies away. In other re-spects, their attack could become a way to enhance our union to God: "Jesus was led up by the Spirit into the wilderness to be tempted by the devil" (Mt 4:1). It was in this confrontation that he manifested his filial connection. Yes, "...the LORD your God is testing you, to know whether you indeed love the LORD your God with all your heart and soul" (Deut 13:3).

Oh eternal Trinity, fire,
abyss of charity....
Could you give me any more
than give yourself to me?
You are the fire that burns forever
and never goes out.
You are the fire that consumes the
soul's self-love.
You are the fire that melts all ice.
You enlighten...
(O, 10).

(To souls given to you):
not only do you give yourself
(as nourishment),
but you also fortify them against
the devil's assaults,
persecutions of the creatures,
the upheavals of their own flesh,
and against the causes
of the problems
and sadnesses from any source.

The wisdom of your Son
enlightens them
through the knowledge
of their inner selves,
of your truth and Satan's deceptions.
The fire of your Holy Spirit
illuminates in their hearts
the desire to love you and
to follow you in truth,
each one more or less,
according to the amount of love
they put in coming to you…
(O, 14).

REFLECTION QUESTIONS

Is my soul aflame for God? Do I fill my mind with ideas for acts of charity? Do I fill my heart with love for God? If I can make an effort to do this, I can live my life in God's peace, leaving no room for the devils, demons, and doubts to enter into my life and make their home.

DAY ELEVEN

"Come Down From Your Cross!"

FOCUS POINT

It was the great love of Jesus Christ for humanity—everyone, everywhere—that kept him on his cross. The will of the Father, that the Son should be sacrificed for the salvation of the beloved men and women of the earth, was the narrow path that was taken. The alluring and wide path of temptation offered by Satan and those who taunted our Lord at the foot of the cross were of no avail then, and are no closer to success today.

"You know that I then showed you myself under the figure of a Tree, of which you saw neither the beginning nor the end, so

that you did not see the roots were united with the earth of your humanity. At the foot of the Tree, if you remember well, there was a certain thorn, from which thorn all those who love their own sensuality kept away, and ran to a mountain of Lolla, in which you did figure to yourself all the delights of the world. That Lolla seemed to be of corn and was not, and, therefore, as you did see, many souls there died of hunger, and many, recognizing the deceits of the world, returned to the Tree and passed the thorn, which is the deliberation of the will. Which deliberation, before it is made, is a thorn which appears to man to stand in the way of following the Truth. And conscience always fights on one side, and sensuality on the other; but as soon as he, with hatred and displeasure of himself, manfully makes up his mind, saying, 'I wish to follow Christ crucified,' he breaks at once the thorn, and finds inestimable sweetness, as I showed you then, some finding more and some less, according to their disposition and desire" (D, 123).

T o let go, to abandon? Temptation is a path, gentle or steep, that takes me further away from Christ. For Catherine, the source of all surrender to temptation is sensuality—the inclination to live according to my own pleasure and avoid suffering. It is an existence that is dominated by the desire to conserve one's life and by the fear of giving it up. The instinct for conservation and pleasure is a gift from God. But it could be turned against the Creator and against ourselves. The Tempter uses it to restrain our freedom, making us believe that we are free of everything and the center of it all.

In the midst of tribulations and those of her disciples, Catherine connected herself more to Jesus' temptations on the cross than to the ones he experienced in the wilderness. They are the same in any event: "the devil departed from him until an opportune time" (Lk 4:13). He incited Christ to find an easier way to fulfill his mission. The same was true for the disciples. On the cross, at the time of his greatest anguish, Jesus was surrounded by people who insulted him: "Come down from your cross!" (Mt 27:40). Abandoned by everyone, he was pushed to abandon everything. "If you are the Son of God, get yourself out of this. Find another way to save us. Give us a sign: throw yourself down!" Jesus would not follow his own inclinations any more than when Satan proposed that he reveal himself by inviting him to throw himself down in the temple.

"Come down from your cross!" (L, 195). Catherine knew this challenge. She knew how much her disciples were exposed to it. The ridicule that accompanied Jesus at the most poignant moment of the gift of himself has had repercussions for centuries. The more our life is given over, the more it will be exposed. "Disconnect yourself from faithfulness to the one to whom you were dedicated through baptism, marriage, in the celibacy of love…! All you have to do…is give up on your life's rule, your marriage contract…. Show us a sign of your freedom." This provocation which is relayed to us today through the media is an act of violence. It reduces love to an external obligation that limits our creative freedom. And what if my faithfulness can be held by nothing other than nails? Would it not be better to remove the nails?

By seeing so much abandonment, so many acts of faithfulness without love, and choices dominated by the fear of suffering, Catherine asked: "What held Christ to the cross? It was neither the nails nor the cross that was able to hold the Man-God: it was the bond of love…" (L, 88). The nails which seemed to hold him were, to the eyes of faith, "the keys that open the kingdom to us" (L, 166). On the cross, the Lord freely responded through love to all seductions. It was there that he offered the definitive refusal to the temptation to evade suffering in order to follow his own path.

The provocation to abandonment comes from the Father of Lies. The cross triumphs over the ambiguities of self. It is a sign of the coherence of Christ's entire life with his mission and his offering: "And for their sakes I sanctify myself, so that they also may be sanctified in truth" (Jn 17:19).

To avoid our responsibilities is an art where the world flatters us. Catherine urges us to be perseverant in prayer, trials, and in the mission. She invites us to follow Christ, "who climbed up on the platform of the cross." He "made his body into a book whose letters are so visible that all mankind can read them perfectly, in spite of the weakness of their intelligence and vision. May your soul then read..." (L, 255).

Here, we add the testimony of Paul who was one of her favorite saints ("mio Paoliccio," as she called him): "I want to know Christ and the power of his resurrection and the sharing of his sufferings by becoming like him in his death, if somehow I may attain the resurrection from the dead.... For many live as enemies of the cross of Christ; I have often told you of them, and now I tell you even with tears. Their end is destruction; their god is the belly; and their glory is in their shame; their minds are set on earthly things.... Therefore, my brothers and sisters, whom I love and long for, my joy and crown, stand firm in the Lord in this way, my beloved" (Phil 3:10–11, 18–19; 4:1).

Even if we cannot remain united with Christ at a time of trial, if we detach ourselves from the plant in a gust of wind,

He will never detach himself from our humanity, nor from the cross on which he offered himself with the sovereign freedom of love. He is grafted to our humanity for all time to purify it, and onto the dry wood of our lives so that we may be fruitful.

Oh love, inestimable love,
if at the time when man was
a tree of death,
you had changed him to a tree of life
by grafting yourself onto man
the life....
If then you did that,
you can now save the whole world which
doesn't know to graft themselves to you.

Men concern themselves with death
and sensuality
and no one comes to your fountain
to draw up the Blood to
water his tree.

Oh eternal Truth,
oh inestimable love,
the same way that you
produced for us
the fruit of the fire, love,
light, and the fruit of your
own obedience which made you run,
drunk with love,
to the shameful death on the cross,
and you gave these fruits

in virtue of the graft of your divinity on our
humanity
and from the graft of your body on the wood
of the cross;
as well, the soul could pay attention
only to your glory and the salvation
of souls; it becomes faithful,
prudent, and patient.

I have sinned, Lord,
have pity on me.
Oh eternal Truth, unite yourself,
graft to yourself those you
have given me
and may I love them with
a special love,
so that they will produce
the fruits of life...
(O, 20).

REFLECTION QUESTIONS

What are the temptations in my life that beckon me "Come down from the cross"? Do these temptations promise me an easier life, free from pain and worry? When these temptations come calling, how do I respond? Do I call upon the grace of God to strengthen me against these temptations?

DAY TWELVE

Where Is Your First Love?
A Letter to a Soul in Crisis

FOCUS POINT

There are times in our lives when we flee the very thing that will help us. There are times when we run away from God even though he is the source of all life, and can give us anything we need. We must return to God during these times of infidelity, and pray for the grace to see that it is God who is our first love, the one who gives us all good things, the greatest good of all.

"Who are the enemies of the soul? The chief is self-love, producing pride, the enemy of humility and charity. Impatience is the enemy of patience, disobedience of true obedience; infidel-

ity, fault, presumption, and self-confidence are not in accord with the true hope the soul should have in me. Injustice cannot be conformed to justice, nor imprudence to prudence, nor intemperance to temperance, nor the transgression of the commandments of the order to the perfect observance of them, nor the wicked conversation of those who live in sin to the good conversation of my servants. These are a man's enemies" (D, 306).

Infidelity is our lot in life: a cooling down of our love, the truth becomes more obscure, a deviation of intelligence and behavior, sin.... Abandonment of God affects conjugal fidelity, the fidelity to one's personal vocation, to the Sunday assembly, the love of the Church, and of one's neighbor.

Sometimes we feel lost, inhabited by a feeling of interior emptiness. We sense inner questions about the way we are leading our lives and we flee our milieu and interiority out of the fear that feelings which could upset our existence might come to the surface. We estimate that we could not allow ourselves this luxury and develop the behavior of a refugee, exiled from ourself. All things "that don't go well" are due to circumstances or are other people's fault.

The flight ahead through taking action or behind through despair are proof of what I dare not let enter into my own existence. The access to my self, my fears, and my aspirations, is banned there, through the fear of revealing an inner conflict. I am torn apart by it....

In a letter to a religious brother, who was engaged in a behavior of flight from his vocation, Catherine reminded him just how necessary the flight of faith is in order to know and love the truth: "I can't see how we could have the light of intelligence without the pupil of very holy faith, which is the center of our life." How can we dissipate the cloud of self-love which prevents the truth...from reaching us? We can do it by recognizing our sins and the infinite mercy of God with respect to us. This self-knowledge and knowledge of God's goodness is born from a deep humility and delivers us from the stubbornness which stifles our conscience. "Sin is normal for man, but perseverance in sin belongs to the devil." This long letter (number 153), written in ecstacy, to a religious brother who had left his order, applies to all forms of infidelity. In it, Catherine developed an admirable itinerary for conversion beginning from the harmonics of the stories of Mark and John, about Mary Magdalene's visit to the tomb, the announcement of the Resurrection and Christ's appearance to Thomas.

To facilitate things, we will divide this sequence into five stages:

1. We must go towards the true Jerusalem,
    it is to your holy order that you must go,
    you will find Jerusalem there, the vision of peace,
    that is to say, the peace of your conscience.

2. You will go into the sepulcher
    of knowledge of your self,
    and with Mary Magdalene, you will ask:
    "Who will remove the stone of the monument for me
    for this stone is so very heavy,
    my sin is so considerable,
    that I can't remove it?"
    But as soon as you will have seen
    and confessed your imperfection,

you will see two angels who will push this stone aside.
—Providence will send you the angel of the holy love
and fear of God;
this love is never alone,
but it gives charity for our neighbor to the soul.
—The angel of hatred of sin, that God will also send you
to remove the stone,
will bring you sincere humility and patience.

3. And then, with a firm hope and a living faith,
    we will never leave the sepulcher of
    self-knowledge;
    we will stay there with perseverance, until we find
    the risen Christ in our soul
    through grace.

4. And when we have found him,
    we will proclaim to our brothers,
    who are the solid and gentle virtues,
    with whom we want to dwell always.

5. Then Christ will appear in the soul
    in a tangible way;
    he will allow himself to be touched
    by humble and continuous prayer.
    Such is the way: there is no other.

In stage one, Catherine exhorts her unfaithful disciple to return to his order so as to find the peace of his conscience again. The itinerary of the return involves a real displacement towards the place of original peace that we left through infidelity. It is only there—it is for each of us to see what this "place" means—that we can find it again. There, we will find "the true Jerusalem," the symbol of peace and God's dwelling.

In stage two, Catherine directs the unfaithful soul into the sepulcher of knowledge of self. It is not necessary to re-integrate oneself into one's community; one must again enter into one's self. The room of self-knowledge becomes a sepulcher because, in terms of interior conflicts, it is death that is triumphant. But the sepulcher in "the true Jerusalem" is a symbol for Christ's sepulcher and of the attachment of Mary Magdalene to Jesus that went beyond his death. In the sepulchre of self-knowledge, it is then the beloved that we seek. Sin has made us weak and powerless. With Mary Magdalene, we ask: "Who will roll the stone aside for us?" Who will give us access to the very depths of ourselves, there where Christ was "dead and buried"? He was dead because of us. He dies for us and for our salvation.

Why is this stone so heavy to remove? Because the weight of lies and the burden of my sins overwhelm me. "Yes, my sins submerge me, their weight is so heavy it crushes me. I admit my sins, my sins frighten me. Make haste to help me, oh Lord, my salvation!" (see also Ps 38). I am so afraid to lose the image I have of myself: I am faced with a roadblock.

When I recognize my fragility and admit my sins, providence will send me two angels. One brings me God's love as well as charity for my neighbor; that is to say, the grace to love those I will find again after having hurt them through my infidelity.

The other angel brings me hatred (of sin) and the grace to become humble and patient.

To put ourselves "in order" is not sufficient to set ourselves straight! The stone of sin must be rolled away with humility and patience. Love and hate are the two faces of the same root. This firmness about conversion comes from grace. By confessing my sins, I draw the grace which delivers me from feelings of power-lessness, which are destructive to myself and others.

The risen Christ in my sepulcher? He is not a stranger to my happiness!

In stage three, we reside in the sepulcher of self-knowledge and, with a firm hope and a living faith, we decide to seek truth, without which there is no faithfulness. "You want truth at the very depth of me; in secret, you teach me wisdom" (see also Ps 51). With perseverance, I remain in the sepulcher of self-knowledge until grace will be given to me: the grace to find Christ again, arisen in my soul. This patience is nourished by an unshakable hope and a living faith. "I anticipate the dawn and I beg. I hope...my eyes anticipate the end of the night.... Lord, you are near" (see also Ps 119).

Perseverance is very important because the danger which lurks over the converted sinner is that the sinner may become presumptuous again. Perseverance is a sign of my humility; through it, I renounce imposing myself on others, making them comply to my schedule; I let my own self-love settle to the bottom and adopt an attitude of waiting. How else can we "understand one another"?

In the fourth stage, we proclaim the Good News to our com-munity, just as Mary Magdalene ran to proclaim the news to the apostles. To evangelize them, I must also evangelize my-self; I proclaim the Resurrection "to my brothers who are the solid and gentle virtues, with whom I want to always dwell." Christ's death had depressed the apostles. Death in the soul dismembers me: withdrawal, interior babbling, and a flow of painful memories; the rift with others widens. In the light of the resurrection, I evangelize myself by dwelling within the solid fundamentals of my life: hope, faith, and charity.

In stage five, Christ appears in a way that allows himself to be touched. In her *Dialogue*, Catherine spoke of the necessity of again finding the unity between the memory of God's benefits which nourish hope—enlightened intelligence through faith—and the will driven by charity. Christ said: "When these three virtues and powers of the soul are gathered together, I keep myself in their midst through grace" (D, 51 and 54; see also Mt 18:19). Here, Christ "appeared in a tangible way and allowed himself to be touched," no longer by Thomas's disbelief, but by faith, through the humble and continuous prayer of the converted sinner. The one who makes himself sensitive to my soul, presents himself to me as sensitive to my prayers.

Catherine concluded: "Such is the way: there is no other."

REFLECTION QUESTIONS

When I have been unfaithful to God by choosing a good that is not the greatest good (that is, God) am I, after some reflection, able to return to God with a humble heart and seeking his mercy? Do I regard God as my first love, the originator of everything which I hold dear—life, family, love? Do I pray for the grace to stay in God's love, hoping never to stray from his presence?

DAY THIRTEEN

To Love "Blood for Blood"

FOCUS POINT

We are cleansed by the blood of Christ. By the blood Christ shed on Calvary we are made clean. We are baptized in the river of Christ's blood. Catherine's "blood imagery" can be shocking, especially to those who are squeamish at the sight or thought of blood. But the imagery is clear, making a strong impression in our thoughts and in our hearts: the fact that Christ shed blood—as the sacrificial lamb for sinful human-ity—on our behalf should never be forgotten.

"Yet let's take heart, my brothers! Our sin, or any diabolical illusion or temptation, however repulsive, filthy, and ugly it may be, need not make us falter; for our doctor has given us a medicine for any sickness we may have. I mean the baptism of

blood and of fire in which the soul cleanses and washes away
every sin, consumes and burns away every diabolical tempta-
tion and illusion—for the fire is steeped in blood, so it truly
does burn" (L, 54).

W ho amongst us is not a bit shy at Catherine's usage
of the word *blood*? The majority of her letters begin
with: "I write to you in his precious blood...." That's enough
to curb our appetite!

Everyone understands the phrase, *to hate blood for blood.*
Our video stores are filled with stories which have the taste for
death which draw their devotees. This is without taking occult
practices into account which handle human and animal blood
in their urban rituals of clairvoyance. Current events and televised newscasts endlessly feed us life and death images and
often gratuitous violence.

Blood is very present in our culture. It is a part of our
modernism. And at the same time, it is unaccepted in our Christian culture: at least there, let us be "clean"! In many ways, we
have difficulty accepting Good Friday. Would Sunday and the
Eucharist still have the same meaning without this exalted
position of faith? Wouldn't the wounds of the risen Christ then
only be simply stage make-up?

What do we do with Christ's open side which the mystics
have contemplated with such ardor? Is it not out of place? In
fact, there is a displacement. Today's man would like us to be
interested in his own wounds, longing for a loving heart to
listen to him and cover his hidden scars, which made him ill,
with the oil of our attention.

Catherine closely examined the mystery of Christ who took

our infirmities upon himself in order that they may be healed by
the grace of his wounds (see also Isa 53:4). He is a doctor for
sinners—he assumes our infirmities in order to make us well:

> *By making yourself small,*
> *you made man big;*
> *saturated with shame,*
> *you filled him with blessings;*
> *by stripping yourself of life,*
> *you have clothed him in grace;*
> *by being covered with shame,*
> *you gave him honor;*
> *stretched out on the cross,*
> *you embraced him*
> *and you made a cavern for him*
> *in your side*
> *so that he will find a refuge in the*
> *face of his enemies.*
> *There, he will find the bath*
> *in which he washed*
> *away the leper of sin from*
> *the face of his soul*
> *(O, 12).*

This language is very poetic because it is filled with love. There
is nothing dry or flat in it, it promotes energy. It places us
before the Word made flesh. Is this linguistic style about flesh
and blood "too strong"? The apostles would be scandalized
by it (Jn 6:60–62)!

While the fans of bloodbaths are sitting in their theater

seats or on their sofas, Catherine invites her disciples to bathe themselves in Christ's blood. "Wash the face of your soul often with confession and penitence of heart.... Enclose yourself into the tender bridal suite, that is to say, in the side of the crucified Jesus, where you can bathe yourself in his blood which has been shed to wash the leper of your soul" (L, 322). A woman is paralyzed by the consciousness of her misery. Catherine exhorts her to stop looking at herself and dwelling on her resentment. What is the cure? Take a good bath! "I truly believe that it is in the remembrance of his blood that we will find the fire of ardent charity, the only thing that is able to remove trouble and bitterness.... Oh glorious and precious blood, you wanted to be a bath for us and an ointment for our wounds! And it is truly a bath, my daughter, since it is in a bath that you find warmth; in the same way, in this glorious bath, you will find the warmth of divine charity."

The blood that is shed for us is not the blood of just anyone: "Know that if he had simply been a man and not God, his blood would have had no value." It is through the union of the divinity to our humanity that Christ's blood has become the river of infinite mercy. "In him we have redemption through his blood, the forgiveness of our trespasses, according to the riches of his grace that he lavished on us" (Eph 1:7–8).

Catherine bathed in the charity that pushed Christ to shed his blood "for the many for the forgiveness of sins" (Mt 26:28). All of her letters begin with the same musical tone: "I write to you in his precious blood!" She addresses each of us more through the love of Christ than through the human love that she brings to us. Our language often limits us in the expression of our feelings and our passions: "There is bad blood between us" or "My blood ran cold!" Catherine wrote in her blood for Jesus, she sees us from the viewpoint of the love that God brings us and not with reference to herself. It is another way of seeing things. It is also a guarantee of her decentering and discernment.

There is a great deal of rapture in Catherine's language because rapture, like foolishness, is a part of love. "Oh foolish love," she said to God! In fact, the one who is enraptured no longer thinks of himself, he sees nothing other than his beloved. Nothing else matters to him. "Enrapture yourself with the blood of the crucified Christ...don't take just a little but a great deal, so that you get drunk and lose yourself" (L, 319). "The blood heats up and destroys all weakness, rejoices the soul and the heart, because it has been shed with the fire of divine charity. The human being that drinks of it will come to a point that he no longer can see himself for himself, he sees himself for God. He sees God, for God, and the neighbor for God" (L, 157).

Christ "jousted with death" until he lost himself for us, "May your heart not resist; may your soul yield because the fire has been set everywhere." That is the rapture that overtook the apostles on the day of the Pentecost. The world believed them to be "drunk" (Acts 2:15). Filled with God's love, they no longer feared losing their self-love, their goods, their consolations, their health, or their lives. To be associated with Christ through the gift of ourself until death is the most noble way to follow him and give him thanks. "You cannot give such a love to me as you have given witness to, but I have given you the mediation of your neighbor so that you can do for him all that you cannot do for me." It is with this dynamic idea that Catherine invites all civil and ecclesiastic leaders, her disciples, and all baptized Christians, to love God and serve the common good; to be ready, if necessary, to give their lives, "blood for Blood" (L, 37), in gratitude for the One who loved us first.

Give thanks for your baptism: "...all of us who have been baptized into Christ Jesus have been baptized into his death" (Rom 6:3) so that our lives would no longer be centered on ourselves.

Bathe in Christ's mercy, in the sacrament of reconciliation. If lukewarmness has won you over, you will find warmth there.

Nourish yourself with his body and blood, the price of your freedom, the source of justice, the strength of the martyrs and the promise of eternal life. You will receive everything "from his blood." And gratitude will enrapture you.

REFLECTION QUESTIONS

When I pray, do I often dwell on thoughts of Christ's suffering, his wounded side, the crown of thorns, the nail marks in his hands and feet? What benefit might there be to a method of prayer that contemplates the precious blood of Christ, blood shed on my behalf, for love of me, and love of the Church?

DAY FOURTEEN

For the Love of the Church

FOCUS POINT

When we consider the tremendous debt that has been forgiven us by God through the sacrifice of his Son, we cannot help but be filled with a love that seeks to share itself with the entirety of humankind. When we are filled with God's love we are moved to let others know what this love is like, and we do our best imitation of Christ's love to give others a taste of what we've come to know of God.

"Dearest father, give a little thought to your perilous state! In what great danger you are, drowning in this bitter sea of deadly sin. Don't we really believe that we must eventually come to the moment of death?... And then that poor wretched soul— who mirrors the carnal pleasures in which he wallows like a

pig in mud—changes from a person into an animal wallowing in putrid avarice. Many times in his greed and avarice he sells spiritual gifts and graces. He becomes swollen with pride, and spends his whole life seeking honor. And what should be given to serve the poor he spends on banquets and a host of servants" (LT).

In the preceding letter, Catherine writes to a parish priest of Asceano. She speaks forthrightly about priestly abuse in the Church which she loved.

Catherine was only six years old when the Lord appeared to her, clothed in the pope's emblems and surrounded by Peter, Paul, and John, above St. Dominique's Church in Siena. The impact of this vision was progressively seen in the form of her vocation: in general, her Dominican spirituality and, above all, her love for the Church, symbolized by the three apostles, and, in particular, her devotion to the pope, in whom she recognized "the tender Christ on earth," as she called him.

In a letter to Nicolas d'Osimo, the secretary and pro-notary of both Pope Gregory XI and Pope Urban VI, she described her love for the Church in order to encourage her correspondent to have as much love. Speaking about herself, she said: "Once, this servant of God ardently wanted to give her blood, to destroy and consume everything that was within herself to be the Bride of Christ, for the holy Church" (L, 85). Then she described the path by which this love is born. As always, she began from the interior room. Through her intelligence, she tried to understand her nothingness and the goodness of God with respect to her. Seeing that God, through love, had given her an existence, and all the graces, all the gifts that he had added, she perceived only one way to thank him: by loving him in return. But how to manifest this love when she could not be useful to God in anything? Finally, she appeared to have found it. She sought to love someone that God loved and for whom she could express her love: the human person. Through love and service to man, she then found the way to show God how much she loved him. Thus, she could give love for Love.

She dedicated herself then to the salvation of her neighbors, and was ready to give her life to obtain it. In this, she imitated the Word made flesh who gave himself for the salvation of everyone. To love the Church is to love it like Christ loved it and give herself for it. Catherine was ready to give her life when it was her turn, to then die to herself.

Hardened by the grace of an exceptional intimacy with the Lord, she saw with so much more acuity that many vocations were not founded on Christ and were weakened by the spirit of the world. She was sick about the condition of the Church. But the Lord taught her that she, herself, had "an occult illness" (D, 108) of which she was not conscious: the one in which she judged the Church and its ministers from her own viewpoint. Catherine had to learn to assess the priests not for what they did —they sinned—but for what they were from Christ's viewpoint: "They are my holy oils and my suns"; they spread the warmth of divine love through the sacraments, no matter how undignified their behaviors may be. At that level, she could not judge them. Catherine set out to present them to the Lord "by addressing him with humble and continuous prayers," so that he would sanctify them. She said: "The soul which totally immerses itself in God is so transformed by God that all of its intelligence, love, and memories are totally in God and concern themselves only with him. The soul neither sees nor thinks of itself or anything other than God" (LM I, 10).

To see the Church "in God" did not stop Catherine from reproaching it about many of the things that still bother us today, because feelings of sadness, like Christ's reproaches to his people, can co-exist with increased tenderness. Her criticisms were not demoralizing, like those that are born from self-love and a blind perception of the Church, which lead to another form of tyranny. Catherine saw the sinful situation of the Church in the light of God's foolish love and Christ's passion for our salvation.

She loved the Church to the point of wanting to suffer and die for it, for its reform and for its unity. She offered herself so frequently because the Church was literally anemic: "The Bride is pale," spiritually and morally weakened. It was contested everywhere and, since the year 1378, it was torn from top to bottom between two popes: Urban VI in Rome and Clement VII in Avignon. Catherine suffered from a lack of holiness, as much for herself as for the hierarchy and the faithful. She rallied herself to lead the battle for unity around Urban VI, who was not always a moderate, whom she counseled to surround himself with wise men and contemplatives rather than politicians and scheming cardinals. She and her spiritual family would also live in Rome at the request of the pope. Those who would lead an evangelical and apostolic life numbered about thirty. Every day, in spite of her frail health and fatigue caused by fasting and vigils, Catherine went to pray at the tomb of Saint Peter. That was her way of "rowing" in the apostle's boat. In the old basilica, Giotto's mosaic, "La Navicella," shows the Church in a storm. On the 29th of January, 1380, Catherine had a vision. She felt the boat of the Church on her shoulders. Under its weight, she buckled. The disciples thought that she was dead. In this interior agony, Catherine felt responsible for the dramatic situation of the Church. She communed with Christ's passion.

On April 29, 1380, Catherine died, surrounded by her disciples, including her mother. She never stopped commending each of her disciples to God, begging forgiveness for her sins and praying for the Church. She said: "Be assured that if I die, the only reason for my death is the love of the Church which enflames and consumes me."

Eternal Father,
I lift my voice to you,
so that you are merciful to
this poor world,
give it the light it so needs
to acknowledge your vicar
(Urban VI).
You have granted him a
naturally virile heart:
oh well, may his courage now be
seasoned with your holy humility.
Take my life, do with it what
pleases you,
from now on and forever.
I dedicate it to your glory,
by humbly beseeching you,
by virtue of your passion,
to purify your Bride of her dirtiness
(O, 28).

Hold vigil over my sons.
Do not leave them orphans.
May your grace visit them.
Join them together with the
tender bond of charity,
so that they will die out of love
for this tender Bride.
I beg you, eternal Father,
not one amongst them
be removed from my care.
Forgive all our iniquities.
And for me particularly,
forgive my ignorance,
forgive the negligence of which
I have become guilty
towards the holy Church.
I am far from having done
all that I could and should have
for the Church.
Lord, I have sinned,
have pity on me!
(O, 29).

REFLECTION QUESTIONS

How do I share God's love with the Church? In what ways do I imitate the love of God for his people in my own life? In what different ways can I try to bring God's love to my neighbor? Am I critical of the Church in some respects? If so, what actions do I seek to take to bring the Church closer to God?

Mary, the Carrier of the Fire

FOCUS POINT

In Mary, the intimacy between Creator and creature was re-born—lost since the Fall in Eden. Catherine, in the same way (if not to the same degree as Mary), felt a strong relationship between herself and the Holy Trinity. We, too, can feel the divine burning within us, for—because of Mary and the Incarnation—we now share in this intimacy of Creator and creature.

"I have not forgotten the reverence and love he [the Father] had for Mary, my only-begotten Son's most gentle mother. For my goodness, in deference to the Word, has decreed that anyone at all, just or sinner, who holds her in due reverence will never be snatched or devoured by the infernal demon. She is

like a bait set out by my goodness to catch my creatures" (D, 139).

―――――――――

C atherine was born on the 25th of March, 1367, on the feast day of the Annunciation. Her life appeared as if it was modeled by the great mystery of the Lord's Annunciation. Like Mary, proportionately speaking, God attracted her with a special love and found himself "inclined to come into her." Following Mary's example, Catherine became the spokesperson of the Word, the carrier of the fire, the distributor of peace, fertile ground and the temple of the Holy Trinity. On the 25th of March, 1379, her loved ones gathered her prayers which were her own Magnificat for the work of salvation. That was one year before she would enter into her full intimacy with God where she continues to intercede for us to this day.

Catherine implores Mary "boldly," through resentment for—or because of—her indignity and sinful state. The "today of God" is more important than the past. "Oh Mary, isn't it just today that the Savior has been seeded in the fertile ground of your womb? (…) I boldly ask you this: it is the day of grace."

In Mary, everything was set up for the welcome: "Temple of the Holy Trinity, fertile ground, vessel of humility, you are the tablet on which is etched…." And everything was set up to give: "Carrier of the fire, distributor of mercy, you made the divine fruit grow, distributor of peace, chariot of fire, you carried the hidden fire, you give us the bread, made from your flour." These expressions have a meaning that is ministerial, active, and dynamic.

Mary was not looked at for herself but contemplated through her relationship with the Holy Trinity as its temple and with all of humanity. That is exactly what was expressed by Vatican II. Mary is not the center of prayer. She is not the sun; she received the light of the sun. She holds a special place; she is the servant of God. Catherine saw her like a parabolic antenna, always oriented towards God and man: the Holy Trinity's plans were what was important...and the extraordinary dignity of the human being.

This prayer leads us directly to the heart of God. In God, "nothing is lacking" and yet: "Oh eternal Trinity, love compelled you to draw man to your heart."

Catherine was marveled by the transcendence of man who "was drawn to the womb of the Holy Trinity" and by God's gracious condescension which created the body of the Word in the womb of his creature.

In God's eyes, Mary had an irresistible charm. There was a mutual attraction. Catherine didn't say it in the same way as did Saint Luke ("You have God's favor. The Lord is with you.") because those words correspond to the language of vocations and missions. She said: "The Lord raptured you...your humility and charity attracted the divinity and made it inclined to come into you." That is why she concluded: "I know that nothing is refused to you." By this mutual attraction, the Creator was smitten with his creature. We may say, "those who believe they are taken, have been." For, by drawing his creature to him, God found himself drawn by her. And, even better, he was "inclined to come into her." Decidedly, he had an inclination....

The bond of intimacy between God and man, broken by sin, was renewed in Mary. In her, the incarnate Word received "the bread made of her flour" so that the divinity would be united and kneaded with humility and "nothing, not death, nor our ingratitudes, could break the union apart...blush my soul" at this admirable lineage, for "this day, this intimate lineage has been contracted with God, which henceforth remains eternally indissoluble."

Mary welcomed the Word with little doubt that all kinds of marvels were possible with God, she remained awestruck before his great goodness. Catherine was marveled as well and, in Mary, admired "the signature" of astonishing human dignity: "You are the book, Oh Mary.... Today, the wisdom of the eternal Father is written in you. Yes, human dignity appears in it, for if I consider you, Oh Mary, I see that the hand of the Holy Spirit wrote the Holy Trinity there. If I consider your great plan, eternal Trinity, I understand that, in your light, you have seen the dignity and nobility of the human race and as love compelled you to draw man from your womb, this same love again compelled you to redeem him when he would be lost."

God tactfully requests Mary's participation in the salvation story. In a sense, "Mary was the redeemer of humankind." Assuredly, Christ is the only Redeemer, but Mary's co-operation appeared at key moments in the history of salvation: the Annunciation, the Incarnation, and the Redemption of man by Christ. "Christ became the Redeemer by his passion; you by the pain in your body and soul."

Saint Luke explained that God did nothing without Mary's consent. Catherine was marveled by the tactfulness of the All-Powerful before the mystery of our freedom: "The eternal Father knocked at the door of your will, Oh Mary, and if you had not wanted to open it, God would not have become incarnate in you." Our consent, primarily in times of difficulty, is generally perceived as a sign of weakness. In fact it is, when we yield to the strongest pressure. But what strength is not expressed when it opens the door with an authentic sense of interior freedom?

The Virgin's consent expresses the co-operation between the finite freedom of the creature and the infinite freedom of its Creator: "It was to these signs that man's dignity appeared...in you today, oh Mary, his strength and freedom appears. For the Word would not have come into your womb if you had not freely consented to it; he (the angel) waited at the door of your will until it pleased you to open it to the one who wanted to come into you." For that is "striking proof of human freedom and strength which nothing could reduce, neither good nor evil, without one's consent."

Was Mary passive in the work of salvation? Not at all: "(the Word) would not have entered if you had not let him in." It was Mary who had the key! Mary had the freedom to say "yes." The one which the icons celebrate as "the door to heaven," Catherine saw as the door of humanity before which God awaits. God knocked at his servant's door! The "yes" to the Annunciation takes its source in Christ's "yes" to his Father's will. And the Father's will is to be merciful to us.

I have recourse to you, Oh Mary, and I pray
to you for the gentle Bride of your most
gentle Son and for his vicar here below,
for those who you,

yourself made me love with
a special love and
for those you have given me.
Mary, carrier of the fire...
chariot of fire....
Inflame their hearts,
make burning coals of them, emblazoned
with the fire of your love and love for their
neighbor.

REFLECTION QUESTIONS

Am I aware of the deep intimacy I have with the Divine? Do I consider the great love of the Blessed Virgin Mary when she consented to be the Mother of God, allowing her womb to be the new Garden of Eden where Creator and creature would be united, and setting in motion the Incarnation that makes possible our intimate participation with the Divine? Do I share the Christ inside of me with all those I encounter?

Bibliography

Baldwin, Anne B. *Catherine of Siena: A Biography*. Huntington, Indiana: Our Sunday Visitor. 1987.

Catherine of Siena, Saint. *The Dialogue*. Translation and Introduction by Suzanne Noffke. Classics of Western Spirituality Series. New York: Paulist Press. 1980.

Catherine of Siena, Saint. *The Letters of St. Catherine of Siena*. Translated with an Introduction by Suzanne Noffke. Binghampton, N.Y.: Center for Medieval and Early Renaissance Studies, 1988.

Cavallini, Giuliana. *Things Visible and Invisible: Images in the Spirituality of St. Catherine of Siena*. Translated by Sister Mary Jeremiah. New York: Alba House, 1996.

De Wohl, Louis. *Lay Seige to Heaven: A Novel About Saint Catherine of Siena*. San Francisco: Ignatius Press, 1991.

Fatula, Mary Ann. *Catherine of Siena's Way*. Wilmington, Delaware: Michael Glazier, 1987.

Jeremiah, Mary. *The Secret of the Heart: A Theological Study of Catherine of Siena's Teaching on the Heart of Jesus*. Front Royal, Virginia: Christendom Press, 1995.

Meade, Catherine M. *My Nature Is Fire: St. Catherine of Siena*. New York: Alba House, 1991.

Noffke, Suzanne, *Catherine of Siena: Vision Through a Distant Eye*. Collegeville, Minnesota: Liturgical Press, 1996.

O'Driscoll, Mary. *Catherine of Siena: Passion for the Truth, Compassion for Humanity.* Selected Spiritual Writings. New Rochelle, N.Y.: New City Press, 1993.